MANFRED VON
RICHTHOFEN

DAVID BAKER

· OUTLINE PRESS ·

This book is dedicated
to the memory of
General Sir Henry Rawlinson

AN OUTLINE PRESS BOOK

Copyright © DAVID BAKER 1990
First published in Great Britain in 1990 by
Outline Press (Book Publishers) Limited
115J Cleveland Street
London W1P 5PN
ISBN 1.871547.06.7

This book was designed and produced by
THE OUTLINE PRESS

Typesetting by Midford Typesetting Ltd.

Printed and bound by Grafoimpex, Zagreb, Yugoslavia.

DESIGN	*Nigel Osborne*
EDITOR	*Sarah Baker*
ARTWORK	*Mike Roffe*
PHOTOGRAPHY	*Mathew Chattle*

Contents

INTRODUCTION *Manfred von Richthofen*

This book about Germany's top scoring air ace of World War I does not purport to be the definitive work on Manfred von Richthofen. Such a book will never be written because there is much uncertainty about his life and exploits that can now never be resolved. The mists of time have folded forever on significant aspects of this man and his activities and key people have long since died or been killed.

What this book does, however, is bring together known facts and personal anecdotes to create a picture very different from the myth that has surrounded this man for more than 70 years. What is known about Manfred von Richthofen is recorded here as the result of much research over many years. There is no end to this absorbing activity an enthusiasts, specialists and historians around the world continue to provide new information about von Richthofen and German aviation on a regular basis.

Among organisations in the forefront of this activity are the Cross & Cockade Society, Cragg Cottage, The Cragg, Bramham, Wetherby, West Yorkshire, England LS23 6QB, and Albatros Productions Ltd, 10 Long View, Berkhampstead, Herts, England HP4 1BY. Both organsations are dedicated to the publication of new material written by ex-World War I aviators and modern resarchers, one for historical detail and the other specially for modellers. Cross & Cockade publish a journal four times each year while Albatros produce a bi-monthly magazine for modellers. Albatros also publish an occassional series of monographs on aircraft and aces of World War I.

Many people have helped in the preparation of this book and the author would like to express his special thanks to them. Most notable was the contribution made by Timothy Graves,who first suggested the idea of a book on von Richthofen and who contributed most of the combat reports and some of the pictures. The author would also like to acknowledge quotations from the English translation of Der Rote Kampfflieger by Stanley M. Ulanoff and published in 1969 by Bailey Brothers & Swinfen Ltd. Also, The Red Knight of Germany by Floyd Gibbons published by Cassell & Co. Ltd., in 1930.

Special thanks must also go to the Royal Air Force Museum at Hendon, England, and to the Imperial War Museum, London. Also to Alex Imrie for some of the photographs and to Mike Roffe for his superb artwork. The content would not have been as comprehensive without the tireless support of the publishers Nigel Osborne and Peter Owen, or as lucid without the editing skills of my wife Sarah, without whom the project would never have reached fruition.

❝ Nothing happens without God's will. This is the only consolation which we can put into our soul during this war. ❞ Manfred Freiherr von Richthofen

CHAPTER ONE *To War*

On a small tributary of the river Oder in south-west Poland lies the ancient town of Schweidnitz. Of strategic importance from ancient times when it was the crossing point for two long distance roads, it has strong military connections. In the 13th century it became a garrison town, diversifying into commerce a century later. Famous first for its beer, then hemp and metal industries, it was also the birthplace of Manfred Freiherr von Richthofen, most recent in a long line of von Richthofens that pre-date the fortress at Schweidnitz itself.

Schweidnitz was a small town; less than 30,000 inhabitants lived out their tranquil lives in what was, for its size, a relatively busy thoroughfare at the end of the last century. With a railway junction for Polish traffic, it was once the part of Europe called Prussia where aristocratic families vied with each other for the quality of their pedigree, the range of their familial associations and the importance of their place in society. It was into this culture that Manfred von Richthofen was born a hundred years ago. A world bounded on one side by the states of ancient teutonic knights and on the other by a feudal wasteland dominated by a Romanoff autocracy.

Manfred von Richthofen was to grow up in this last bastion of Imperial Germany to become the greatest fighting airman of World War I. He was an enigma, rarely exposing his character or personality to friends or fellow aviators and he became a living legend, much of the mystery with which he surrounded himself remaining today. Yet strip away that facade and a very real person emerges. Not an automaton bent on killing his fellow man for the sake of it as some would have had us believe.

Rather, a patriotic German serving his kaiser, his country and his family in a war all men thought would be the last ever fought.

Of course, none of his later glory was suspected when Baroness Kunigunde von Richthofen gave birth to her son that quiet spring day in the last decade of the 19th century. Born on May 2, 1892, Manfred was to be the eldest of three boys born to the Baroness and Rittmeister Albrecht Freiherr von Richthofen. Lothar would be born on September 27, 1894, followed by Karl Bolko in 1903. Manfred and Lothar would serve with distinction in the Great War to end all wars and both would die while flying aeroplanes, one in 1918, the other in 1922.

Descended from a family of Prussian junkers, the von Richthofen name was acquired in the 17th century by decree of Emperor Leopold I who bestowed it upon Johann Praetorius, when three years before his death he became Ritter Johann Praetorius von Richthofen. Johann's grandfather, Samuel Praetorius, was the adopted son of Paulas Schultze who had accepted the name Praetorius from the 16th century Emperor Ferdinand I. Schultze had been a friend of Sebastian Schmidt, adopting Samuel in order to continue the newly acquired family name and fortune. Sebastian and Barbara were financially well rewarded for giving up their son for this dutiful purpose!

As Prussian landowners the von Richthofens had settled in Silesia during the time of Johann and lived the life of gracious aristocrats. As pillars of the German-Austrian alliance they were embraced by Frederick the Great who granted them a knighthood, giving the family the hereditary title Freiherr. In the 19th century one von Richthofen became an explorer in China, four served in the Reichstag and one was Secretary for Foreign Affairs to Kaiser Wilhelm II. Of more lasting association, Frieda von Richthofen, daughter of one Friedrich, caught the attention of the young English writer D. H. Lawrence while on a visit to England in 1912. Infatuated, he pursued her back to Germany and in time she became an inspiration for his literary genius.

In the year Frieda met Lawrence, Manfred passed out as a Lieutenant in the 1st Regiment of Uhlans Kaiser Alexander III, one year after joining the unit from the Berlin War Academy. It was to have been the start of a career in the Army that his father had been unable to pursue due to deafness; a condition brought on by an illness suffered after he dived fully clothed into an icy river to rescue three soldiers from his Leibkurassier Regiment.

"I entered the Cadet Corps as a boy of eleven. I was not particularly eager to become a cadet, but my father wished it and I was not consulted. I found it difficult to bear the strict discipline and order. I did not care very much for the instruction I received, and I was never good at learning things. I did just enough work to pass. In my opinion, it would have been wrong to do more than was necessary, so I worked as little as possible."

1903

Major Albrecht von Richthofen decided when Manfred was a child that his eldest son would have a military career. Brought up in a wealthy German family, Manfred was greatly influenced by the superior position in society held by these teutonic Prussian settlers, albeit two centuries removed. In 1903, at the age of eleven, Manfred was sent to the Military School at Wahlstatt. The hard, disciplinary life style eked out at this school gave Manfred the military bearing in physique and mental commitment that was to characterise his approach to arduous tasks. Frugal living and strenuous physical exercise underpinned long hours of study, with little time for relaxation.

In these years the young boy grew to premature manhood and in so doing became something of a recluse. Denied emotional warmth and home comforts, Manfred disliked his school intensely and on vacation back home cautioned his younger brother Lothar against choosing a military career. Nevertheless, he learned a great deal about the prowess of German armies in the field, about the expectations of an officer and about loyalty, nationalism and tenacity of will. All these things would help shape an almost fanatical resolve to stand firm against challenge, to dedicate effort to success and to maintain a stiff upper lip in adversity.

In several respects the school de-humanised the officers' commitment to their task and de-personalised the business of war. Manfred was thus able to throw himself eagerly into the fray without thought for the consequence to himself or his opponent. This was an arguably desirable asset in aerial combat but another more important skill was essential. He had to be a good shot. Early on he learned to love the chase and thrilled to the tension and challenge of the hunt; he had plenty of opportunity to hone those skills on his parents' estate in Schweidnitz.

After only a year at Military School, Manfred was a keen shot and enthusiastic to use every opportunity to improve his performance. So much so that, failing to find wildfowl to pot at, he raised the domestic ducks to flight and practised on them! His mother was furious but grandmother urged that he should be forgiven. He was to be praised, she said, for having readily admitted guilt and firmly standing his ground. Such were the expected standards of Prussian life that the positive side of this incident, when Manfred exercised his initiative and firmly admitted guilt, significantly outweighed the negative aspect of wanton shooting on the domestic duck population. His mother still had three duck feathers stuck to brown paper with sealing wax long after the war: Manfred's first trophies.

" I liked the school at Lichterfelde much better. I did not feel so isolated from the world, and I began to live more like a human being. My happiest memories of Lichterfelde are those of the great sporting events when my opponent was Prince Friedrich of Prussia. The Prince won many first prizes and other awards higher than mine, as I had not trained as carefully as he had."

1909

Not that rigid military discipline erased every element of humour and boyishness. As he was to recall of these days, **"I had a great liking for risky tricks. One fine day my friend Frankenberg and I climbed the well-known steeple of Wahlstatt by going up the lightning rod. I tied my handkerchief to the top of the steeple. I remember vividly how difficult it had been to negotiate the gutters along the way. Ten years later I visited my youngest brother, Bolko, at Wahlstatt, and I saw my handkerchief still tied high in the air. "**

With a self denigrating frankness not often found among achievers, Manfred affirmed that **"I was never good at learning things. I did just enough work to pass. In my opinion, it would have been wrong to do more than was necessary, so I worked as little as possible. As a result, my teachers did not have a high regard for me. "** This was true in part only, for Manfred excelled at physical sports and was awarded several prizes by the School Commandant for performance on the parallel bars and on the field. He particularly liked group sports like soccer where he could excel among equals. From an early age, Manfred pursued physical fitness, using any excuse to demonstrate prowess. He was never very good at academic subjects and he was not encouraged.

Three years before starting at the Military School, he developed a trick of climbing the highest apple tree on the family estate and, using a low hanging branch, would deftly swing down to the ground in a perfectly executed sequence of movements that left his parents gasping in amazement. From an early age Manfred also had a stoic determination to overcome obstacles. On one occasion his parents were expecting him home from the Military School and sent a boy to meet him at the local railway station. The train came and went but Manfred was nowhere to be seen. After a while he arrived on foot, having walked from the station with two large bags.

After six years at Wahlstatt, Manfred left and moved on to the Royal Military Academy at Lichterfelde where he found life much more to his liking. **"I did not feel so isolated from the world and I began to live more like a human being, "** he would relate with nostalgia. This was just what he needed to convince him that a military career was what he wanted and quite soon Manfred was committed to the notion of becoming a cavalry officer, coupling his love of horses with the dash and flair of life as a lancer.

Manfred was good with horses and used every opportunity he could find to gallop off into the forests of Silesia and pretend he

"One of my military school instructors had bought a nice fat mare named Biffy. Her one defect was that she was about fifteen years old. She had somewhat fat legs, but was otherwise an excellent jumper. I rode her often. About a year later a cavalry captain in the regiment who was a sports enthusiast told me that he had bought a rather clumsy eight year old jumping horse. We were all curious about the 'clumsy' jumper that bore the name Biffy but I certainly did not associate her with the mare of my military school teacher. The day the wonderful animal arrived I was amazed to find that good old Biffy had turned up as an 'eight year old' in the captain's stable. She won more jumping competitions, but she changed masters agin. She was killed at the beginning of the war."

1911

Above
An enthusiastic horseman, Manfred (left) is seen at the horse trials held in Breslau in 1913.

was an important general leading a charging squadron to the fray. Infused with lessons on military strategy, tactics and deployments, and solidly indoctrinated in the objectives of military campaigns, Manfred von Richthofen became an enthusiastic young officer with the 1st Regiment of Uhlans Kaiser Alexander III, receiving his commission in April, 1911. A brief interlude at the Berlin War Academy, where serious business was taught, had finally prepared him for military duty.

On becoming a Lieutenant in 1912, Manfred's father gave him a fine mare which he called Santuzza. The life of a young officer in a regiment of Uhlans required him to excel on horseback and von Richthofen actively participated in jumps and races, gaining several prizes but collecting a broken collar bone in the Kaiser Prize Race of 1913. Shielded from the gathering storm clouds in Europe by a brash enthusiasm for life, Manfred and his fellow officers were unable to reconcile rumours of war with their new found opportunities for relaxation and the fruits of having successfully negotiated the first rungs on a ladder to recognition as professional soldiers.

Only the day before World War I broke out, as Manfred would relate, **"We convinced (ourselves) that war was out of the question and continued our celebration. "** For Lt. Manfred von Richthofen, the prospect of war was not unthinkable but certainly barely considered for was he not about to train his new horse Antithesis for the jumping events that autumn? The rewards for hard school work and graduation into the officer caste put young Manfred's thoughts far from conflict. The mobilisation of Russia put an end to speculation. Germany marched and von Richthofen was at war.

Moved across the border on August 2, 1914, to a location near the Polish village of Kielce, he was soon in action. A near brush with a Cossack patrol was followed by further orders to entrain for what would soon become the Western Front. Clearly, Manfred was emotionally moved by the threat of war. In a letter to his parents dated August 2, he revealed a suspicion that he would not survive the dreadful combat in which he was to play so vital a role: **"These are to be my last lines, written in a hurry. My most hearty greetings to you. If we should never see each other again, take these, my most sincere thanks, for everything you have done for me. I leave no debts behind me. I have, on the contrary, saved a few hundred marks which I am taking with me. "**

Germany was embarked upon a massive series of troop movements, switching vast armies from east to west in an attempt to defeat France and Belgium by wheeling round the North Sea coast and smashing through existing defences. With 1.5 million men on the march, the Kaiser expected to be in Paris within 40 days. Then he would transfer his victorious armies to the Eastern Front, ready to deal with the Russians. So it was that Manfred found himself near the French border marching north toward Luxembourg. **"We continued on through Luxembourg and Esch, and finally approached the first fortified cities of Belgium. "**

Germany had launched its attack on Belgium on August 4, 1914, pushing 60,000 troops through the Liege gateway. Nearly three weeks had gone by and Manfred's attitude had changed. Brother Lothar was in the Dragoner Regiment Nr. 4 and serving on the same front although he would spend the winter on the Eastern Front. Manfred was concerned lest his younger brother distinguish himself first. Suddenly, from the relaxed pleasures of peace the von Richthofens had been hurled into the challenging tensions of war and in 1914 all men naively sought to achieve glory before it was all over.

"My father bought me a beautiful mare called Santuzza. She was the most wonderful animal, virtually indestructible but gentle as a lamb. I discovered she had a great talent for jumping, so I decided to make a jumping horse out of her. I found great sport and much understanding in a comrade named von Wendel, who had won many valuable prizes with his charger Fandango. We both trained for a jumping competition and distance race to be held in Breslau. Fandango trained splendidly and, making great efforts, Santuzza also did well. I had hoped to win some event with her. On the day before she was to be loaded on to the train I could not resist taking her over the hurdles in our training area once more. In so doing we slipped. Santuzza bruised her shoulder and I cracked my collar bone."

Autumn 1912

"I also owned a very good charger, and this unfortunate animal had to do everything: running, distance racing, jumping competition, parade marching. In short, there was no practice in which this fine animal had not been trained. Her name was Flower, and I achieved some very fine wins on her. My last victory was the Kaiser Prize Race of 1913. I was the only one to complete the whole circuit without a mistake. Something happened to me that could not be easily duplicated. I galloped over the heather, and then, suddenly landed on my head. The horse had stepped into a rabbit hole and, in the fall, I had broken my collar bone. I remounted and rode another seventy kilometres with the injury, but finished in good time without making a mistake."

1913

The battle of Verdun is very severe, and day after day a vast number of lives are sacrificed. Only yesterday, eight officers of the Seventh Grenadiers were killed in one attack.

September 1914

When the tortuous realities of deadly conflict replaced this hopeless search for gallant deeds a degree of boredom set in, preceded by a realisation that the war itself would claim many victims before the last shot. For Manfred, boredom was imposed because there were fewer jobs for a cavalry detachment to do in the face of the massive fortifications that confronted the Uhlans at Verdun. The dashing war of cavalry charges, flashing swords and galloping horses had gone. Before the end of 1914 he had received the Iron Cross Third Class for mounted patrols, becoming one of more than five million Germans to carry that decoration. Manfred was relegated to a supply unit and endless paperwork.

There I sat for weeks on end underground in a shell-proof, heated dugout. Back and forth I went taking things here and there. I went uphill, downhill, criss-cross through an unending number of trenches and mudholes until I finally came to where the fighting was going on. Every man had a spade and a pick and gave unending effort to digging as deeply as possible into the ground. It was quite funny that in many places the French were only five paces ahead of us. We heard them talking and smoking cigarettes. Now and then they threw us a piece of paper. After spending a full working day in the stinking trenches bored with the routine of a soldier's life, von Richthofen would steal away in the night hours and crouch in a tree hide waiting for game. Many nights, the future warrior honed his hunting skills and sharpened his senses for the kill that would inevitably came his way.

On through the winter of 1914-15 von Richthofen carried messages, occasionally getting into the fight. Once after dismounting from Antithesis a grenade landed on the saddle killing three other horses and sending a piece of shrapnel ripping through Manfred's cloak without effect on its occupant. In January, von Richthofen wrote home. *I am the Assistant Adjutant of the 18th Infantry Brigade.* He saw more action and was pleased with that but when his unit was sent to consolidate an offensive on the Front Manfred once more found himself on administrative duties. In March, a letter home to his mother was full of joys:

Dear Mamma:

I come with glad tidings. Yesterday I was decorated with the Iron Cross. How are matters around Lemberg? Let me give you some sound advice. If the Russians should come, bury everything you want to see again deep down in the garden, or elsewhere. Whatever you leave behind you will never see again. You wonder why I save so much money, but don't forget that, after the war, I must equip myself again from head to foot. Everything I took with me is gone, lost, burned, torn – not even excluding my saddle. If I should come out of this war alive, I shall have more luck than brains.

late 1914

At last I have found an outlet for my energies. On the days free from trench duty, I go hunting. I am rather proud of my bag of three wild boars. The details of these hunting excursions I am writing to Papa. Three days ago we had a veritable offensive for wild pigs with thirty drivers and five hunters. I myself was the host of the party. The drivers stirred up eight pigs but every one of us missed his game. The affair lasted from eight in the morning till seven in the evening. In three days we will have another try, and in ten days, with a full moon, I am expecting confidently to bag a wild boar. **"**

A month later, Manfred summed up the concerns that wracked the thoughts of most soldiers in that first spring of the war: **"** *Who would ever have thought that the war would continue so long. Everyone believes that we will win, but no one knows when that will be. Consequently, we have to struggle on.* **"** Manfred was not inclined to 'struggle on' and wrote to his Commanding General requesting transfer to the Air Service. There at least, he thought, he would face new and exciting challenges and free himself from the anonymity of routine non-combatant duties.

Of flying, Manfred knew nothing. **"** *I hadn't the slightest idea what our flyers did,* **"** he had mused during the march through Luxembourg in August 1914. **"** *I considered every flyer an enormous fraud. I could not tell if he were friend or foe. I had no idea that German machines bore crosses and the enemy's had cockades.* **"** This effectively summed up the attitude of infantry and cavalry men in 1914 to aviators of the day. Flyers were considered an irrelevant diversion from the real business of war. His application having been approved, the truth would assume grim reality soon enough as he prepared to transfer from the trenches to the air.

" *Dear Mamma:*

At last I have found a sufficient outlet for my energies. On the days free from trench duty, I go hunting. I am rather proud of my bag of three wild boars. The details of these hunting excursions I am writing to Papa. Three days ago, we had a veritable offensive for wild pigs with thirty drivers and five hunters. I myself was the host of the party. The drivers stirred up eight pigs, but every one of us missed the game. The affair lasted from eight in the morning till seven in the evening. In three days we will have another try, and in ten days, with a full moon, I am expecting confidently to bag a wild boar. **"**

March 1915

" *Who would ever have thought that the war could continue so long. Everyone believes that we will win, but no one knows when that will be. Consequently, we have to struggle on.* **"**

April 1915

CHAPTER TWO *Into The Air*

Manfred joined the Flieger-Ersatz-Abteilung Nr. 7 (No. 7 Air Replacement Section) at the end of May 1915, along with thirty fellow officers who would train as observers. The school provided instruction in basic flying principles, explained how engines worked, how cameras took pictures, what the observer had to do to get the best results and what the Army expected from him. As the officer, von Richthofen would be in charge of

" *It never occurred to me to be a pilot. I was anxious to get into the air at the front as quickly as possible. I began to fear that I might get there too late; that the World War would be over before I could really get into it. To become a pilot would have required three months' training, and by that time peace might have been concluded.* **"**

1915

the aircraft. The pilot was the chauffeur. Manfred remembered his first flight well.

*** The night before I had gone to bed earlier than usual to be fresh for the great moment next morning. We drove to the airfield and I sat in a plane for the first time. The blast of wind from the propeller disturbed me greatly. It was impossible to make myself heard by the pilot. Everything flew away from me. My flying helmet slipped off, my muffler loosened too much, and my jacket was not buttoned (sufficiently) securely. In short, I was miserable. Before I knew what was happening, the pilot got the engine up to full speed and the machine began rolling, faster and faster. I hung on frantically. Then the shaking stopped and we were in the air. ***

Like most people experiencing their first flight, it was an unforgettable event. *** I had been told where I was to direct my pilot to fly,*** he would recall later. *** We flew straight ahead for a while, then my pilot made one turn after another, right and left, and I lost all sense of orientation to the airfield. I had no idea where I was. Very carefully I began to look over the side at the ground below. The people looked tiny and the houses looked like something out of a child's toybox, everything was so small and fine. In the background lay Cologne. The Cathedral looked like a plaything. Who could have touched me? No one! I didn't care where I was and I was quite sad when the pilot said he thought we had better land. ***

From the outset, von Richthofen was enamoured with flying. But not as a technical achievement or even for its own sake. Manfred was captured by the opportunities it provided for experiencing a new, elevated detachment from the mud and the boredom of trench warfare.

It gave him for the first time since the opening weeks of war an exhilaration that had been lost when his role in combat as a lancer had been replaced by the new tedium of mechanised conflict and the wearying repetition of administrative and supply duties. Soon, he would aspire to fly and fight at the same time. Here at last was a role with which he could identify, and the emerging cadre of single-seat fighter pilots would lure him to the brotherhood of famous names that gave him added reason to excel.

Above all, Manfred wanted to distinguish himself with honour, preferably in battle, before the war ended. The Prussian upbringing he received both at home and in military school instilled in him a need to exploit opportunities for greatness and distinction. Moreover, his taller, handsome brother threatened his position as senior under their father. If Lothar was able to distinguish himself to a greater extent than he, it would be a matter for real concern! So, with his newly found role, Manfred von Richthofen eagerly sought ways not only to excel but to exceed the prominence his brother might bring to the family.

A few weeks after his first flying experience, Manfred was sent to Grossenhain on June 10 to join Flieger-Ersatz-Abteilung Nr. 6 where he completed his training before assignment to Feldfliegerabteilung Nr. 69 on the Eastern Front. This would be but a brief stay, yet it would give von Richthofen a panoramic view of one of the biggest battles of World War I. For little more than two months he would be carried aloft in two-seat aircraft such as the Albatros B II watching over the vast movements of General von Mackensen's armies. Of those days he would write later, **66 _This was a wonderful time. Life in the Air Service was very much like life in the cavalry. Every day, morning and afternoon, I had to fly reconnaissance missions, to gather valuable intelligence information._ 99**

Von Richthofen had made the transition from horse to aeroplane, returning to perform a similar mission to that for which he had been trained as an Uhlan. It epitomised the onset of a new, mechanised form of warfare where the horse was replaced by the machine. At first he was teamed with Oberleutnant Georg Zeumer, a small, wiry little man wasting toward death by an incurable tuberculosis. Zeumer knew he was dying and daily went to war not caring whether he lived or perished. Distant, drawn and pale-faced with inset eyes that seemed locked on a far horizon, Zeumer had the look and pallor of death. Fired by the grand strategies unfolding far below and motivated with the great sweeps made by von Mackensen's troops as they advanced upon Brest-Litovsk, Manfred sought more dashing company and found it in the motor racing enthusiast, Count Erich Graf von Holck.

Unlike Zeumer, who was one of Germany's earliest pilots, von Holck was young, had just learned to fly, and his confident air of a dashing warrior appealed to Manfred. He arrived at the airfield at Rawa Ruska on foot, having walked thirty miles ahead of the train which carried his baggage and his orderly. Count von Holck treated flying like a sport, an attitude with which Manfred could identify, and boldly thrust forward to new challenges. Here at last, Manfred had found a kindred spirit but the almost reckless abandon with which the two went to war nearly resulted in their deaths on one occasion.

66 Dear Mamma:

I hope you are receiving the letters I am sending. I am here with the Mackensen Army and am attached to the Sixth Austrian Corps. Now we are again in the full movement. Nearly every day I fly over the enemy and report. I reported the retreat of the Russians three days ago. It gives me great fun – at least, more than I have when I play at being an orderly officer. We all live in tents. The houses are nearly all burned down, and the remaining ones are so filled with vermin that no human being can enter them. I am so pleased that I can help here just at the most important sector of the front. In all probability, matters will come to a decision here shortly. I have been flying here now for a fortnight. The period of training lasted for four weeks only. Of my fellow students, I was the first to be sent to a field flying formation. 99

July 20 1915

Flying close to the burning town of Wicznice they headed straight for a rising column of smoke, stoked by fires on the ground that joined in a single conflagration. Blissfully ignorant of the smoke's effect on the dynamics of air and aerofoils, the two intrepid aviators narrowly survived a fiery end when their aircraft fell like a stone to 1,500 feet before von Holck managed to reach clear air. Nevertheless, the engine was faltering and as the aeroplane descended it was hit by machine gun fire from Russian troops.

Seeking a clearing in a forest recently occupied by the enemy, von Holck and Manfred von Richthofen landed roughly and fled for protection from the trees. **66** *When we reached the forest we stopped, and I saw through my field glasses that a soldier was running towards our plane. I was horrified to see that he wore a cap and not a spiked helmet. That was a sure sign he was a Russian. But when the man came closer Holck shouted for joy, for he was a Prussian grenadier guard.* **99**

On August 21, 1915, von Richthofen was sent from the Eastern Front back across Germany to join a bombing unit operating under the code name Brieftauben-Abteilung-Ostende, the Carrier Pigeon Unit at Ostend, on the Belgian coast. It would eventually become Kampfgeschwader Nr. 1 when all pretence of camouflage for its real task was removed. From two-seat reconnaissance aircraft to twin engined bombers, von Richthofen traded cameras for bomb release gear. Once again he was teamed with the ailing Zeumer. Fascinated at first by the limitations of the giant aircraft, Manfred found new exhilaration in watching the results of his bombs exploding on contact with the ground. This was more like the war he had come to fight! But his first war wound was less dramatic. Over enthusiastic to watch the white and grey puffs of smoke bursting from explosions on a village near Dunkirk, Manfred momentarily forgot the close proximity of the whirling propellers. Signalling frantically to Zeumer instructions on how to bank the aircraft and give him a clear view of the ground, Manfred lost the tip of his finger. Several days later, on September 1, 1915, von Richthofen got his first opportunity to shoot at another aeroplane in the air. Sighting a two-seat Farman pusher biplane he signalled to Zeumer to give chase and for a few minutes the two biplanes circled each other. Richthofen got off a few shots and the observer in the Farman put a few bullets through the fabric of the German bomber before making off, much to Manfred's disgust.

A week later, Manfred felt the force of the Royal Navy when warships off the beaches at Ostende bombarded the German positions but aircraft attacked the ships and HMS Attentive received a few direct hits. Yet even in this static war of attrition there was some movement as Manfred noted in his account of this period. *66 The wonderful time in Ostende was very short, for soon the battle in the Champagne region broke out and we flew to this Front in order to play a greater part with our large battle planes. We soon realised that our old packing crate was a grand plane, but it would never make a fighter. 99*

Von Richthofen was itching for adventure and the drudgery of struggling against the wind in an aeroplane with little manoeuvrability and almost no chance of knocking down other aeroplanes bored him. Yet there were opportunities, and during a flight with a pilot named Osteroth, Manfred got another chance to shoot at the enemy. When a Farman biplane hove in sight, Osteroth slowly closed the distance. When close enough to secure a hit, Manfred rattled away with a machine gun from the rear cockpit. Unaware that it was about to be attacked, the Farman had chugged along complacently but now the pilot sought evasive action as the observer returned the fire. Manfred's gun jammed and fearing his prey would escape he worked feverishly to unblock it.

Succeeding, von Richthofen fired another burst before the Farman slowly fell away toward the ground. Astonished at the result of what seemed an effortless battle, Manfred frantically signalled Osteroth to follow it down to where the French biplane lay crushed in a crater, its tail pointing skyward. He never learned whether the crew survived and since the aircraft fell behind enemy lines he was not permitted to claim it as a personal victory. But it was von Richthofen's first, albeit unrecorded, success in air combat although a year would pass before he began his official score card.

On October 1, 1915, von Richthofen was posted along with Zeumer to the other German bombing unit: Brieftauben-Abteilung-Metz, later to become Kampfgeschwader Nr. 2. While Manfred was assigned the observer's seat in a B-class biplane, Zeumer was given one of the new Fokker monoplane scouts. This increased Manfred's frustration. He was determined to learn to fly and assume a more commanding responsibility for air-to-air fights. The new scouts gave a pilot the chance to shoot down enemy aeroplanes in flight without the need of an observer and this was an attractive proposition for the young Prussian. Fitted with a synchronising gear which allowed a machine gun to fire through the propeller arc, the production Fokker monoplanes had entered service during June and the type was to become the scourge of the Western Front.

There were rising stars in the German Air Service who encouraged von Richthofen, men who were shooting down increasing numbers of enemy aircraft and receiving the acclaim of a grateful nation. Soon, their names would be immortalised and Manfred was not to know that he would eventually join their ranks and transcend by his own achievements the envied records of the men whose careers he now followed with great interest. One of these was the likeable Oswald Boelcke who had already shot down four enemy aircraft. Von Richthofen met Boelcke in the dining car of the train that was taking him to his new appointment and boldly asked him why he had been unable to shoot down as many aircraft. Boelcke replied that he would have to fly a Fokker monoplane to do that!

Von Richthofen made his first solo flight on October 10 after the diminutive Zeumer had given his protege twenty-four hours of instruction and deemed his pupil as ready as he would ever be for the all important event. Like his first flight, Manfred was to remember clearly the first time he went into the air alone: **66** *The engine started with a roar. I pressed the throttle and the machine began to pick up speed, and suddenly I could not help but notice that I was really flying.* **99** Manfred found that getting back down on the ground can be a tricky feat to accomplish and although he escaped without injury the severity of the crash landing that ensued when he got it slightly wrong, his aircraft was completely destroyed.

Undeterred, he was back in the air two days later making several successful take-offs and landings and two weeks after that he took his field examination which cleared him to go to a special flying school at Doberitz near Berlin. The neophyte pilot soon struck up a friendship with one Oberleutnant Bodo Freiherr von Lyncker and the two young men conspired to fly Fokker monoplanes in one of the new Kampf und Feldfliegerabteilungen. Special units formed for reconnaissance and fighting, they attracted hunters and pilots in search of adventure. Fast monoplane scouts with two machine guns firing forward, the Fokkers had brought a new dimension to war in the air and von Richthofen and Lyncker vowed to join them.

At Doberitz, von Richthofen went through a rigorous series of flying lessons and performed various tests under strictly controlled conditions contrived to pass him fit for any aeroplane in service. But even the social pressures in Berlin were unable to pull Manfred away from the forests and estates where sport was to be found. On several occasions, von Richthofen incorporated a trip via the Buchow estate into his scheduled flying lessons and spent several hours hunting for wild pig before setting off back

Far Right
Oswald Boelcke was a great inspiration to von Richthofen and taught him well in the two months they flew and fought together in Jasta 2.

Since spending the New Year at Schwerin I have not flown once. It rains incessantly here, and we seem to be making no progress. I should love to be at the front right now. I think there is a lot going on there.

January 11 1916

to the airfield. Finally, on December 25, 1915, Manfred passed his final examination but was not to join an active unit for almost three months.

Meanwhile, he flew around Germany, gaining experience in the air, once landing near his home at Schweidnitz and on a single occasion walking out with his mother in Berlin. Much shorter in stature than his brother Lothar, Manfred was self conscious of his height and bristled when his mother said that more girls looked at Lothar when she walked with him than they did at him when they walked together. Manfred retorted: **I will make more of them look at me one of these days.** Lothar was never shy in a woman's company but Manfred felt uneasy and would physically shift from leg to leg, seeming not to know how to relate to a member of the opposite sex.

That the 23 year old Manfred was uncomfortable in the presence of women, or in the flesh-pots of Berlin, was well known to his fellow pupils at Doberitz and much has been made since of his disinterest in a permanent relationship with a woman. There is nothing, however, to suggest that Manfred was anything other than a sexual recluse and although at most he may have been a misogynist there is no reason to believe his dislike of women was attributable to alternative sexual interests. His closest friends, in fact, saw him as a man who genuinely felt preoccupied with equally basic instincts - of hunting and stalking prey for a clean kill. The truth may have been somewhat more complex.

In March, 1916, more than five months after he left the Western Front to become a pilot, Manfred joined his unit near Verdun. He was again flying Albatros two-seater biplanes, this time in the front seat. The emergence of single-seat fighting scout planes had transformed the original relationship of pilot and observer. Now the pilot was no longer merely the chauffeur but could carve for himself a dashing role. The Albatros observation aircraft, though, was less charismatic, taking almost an hour to reach 10,000 feet – twice as long as it took a Fokker monoplane to reach the same height.

Undeterred, and spoiling for a fight, Manfred had a gun fitted to the upper wing above the forward cockpit of his Albatros biplane, angled upward so that he could fire above the propeller arc. This also enabled him to control the fight from the front! That was at least partial compensation for finding himself without a coveted monoplane to fly. It had become common practice to attach a gun this way and avoid the need for complex synchronising gear which would inhibit it from firing when a propeller blade passed in front of the barrel. Field modifications became quite common in air forces of the fighting powers as ideas evolved more rapidly than they could be formally applied through the production lines.

Manfred got his first chance to fly and fight in the air when his Albatros chanced upon a French Nieuport also equipped with a gun on the upper wing centre-section. But the pilot seemed to be a novice for he shied away from the fight and made a dash for his own side of the lines. In pursuit, Manfred overhauled the reluctant enemy and got close before opening fire. This was to characterise Manfred's fighting tactic when he progressed to single-seat scouts.

On this occasion it was a good omen for the tactic worked and the Frenchman fell away, tumbling down toward the trenches. Like his previous 'victory', this was not accredited to von Richthofen because the wreckage fell near Fort de Douaumont on the Allied side of the line. It was a step toward recognition, however. The communique for April 26 acknowledged that the aircraft had been shot down by a German aircraft, the second of two that day.

On the first day of May 1916, Manfred witnessed the death of his former flying colleague Count von Holck when he saw a tiny Fokker monoplane dive through cloud straight into the ground from 9,000 feet. Two days later he was one of the pilots that flew a salute over Count von Holck's grave. The realities of war on the ground had come home to Manfred more than a year before. The grim face of war in the air was only just emerging. There were threats airmen faced over and above enemy aircraft and their eager crews. The design and construction of aircraft in 1916 was a science still very much in its infancy and airmen knew they were just as likely to be dashed to the ground by fierce storms as they were from a fusillade of bullets. Manfred experienced one such storm that left an indelible impression:

I had never made an attempt to fly through a thunderstorm, but I could not resist experimenting once. Thunder was in the air the whole day. I was at the airfield at Metz and wanted to return to my field. As I pulled my machine out of the hangar the first signs of an approaching thunderstorm became noticeable. The wind blew up the sand, and a pitch-black wall arose from the north. Old, experienced pilots urged me not to fly. I would have appeared timid if I stayed away because of a stupid thunderstorm. Right at the start it began to rain. I had to take off my goggles

Dear Mamma:

In haste – some good news. Look at the communique of yesterday, April 26th. One of these planes was shot down by my machine gun and is to my credit.

April 27 1916

I love my new occupation as a pilot. I don't think anything else can attract me in this war. I fly a Fokker monoplane – a plane with which Boelcke and Immelmann have had great success. I was very much grieved about Holck's death. Three days before he was killed, he visited me and we had much fun together. He told me of his imprisonment in Montenegro. One really cannot imagine that this fine, healthy and strong fellow doesn't exist any more. I witnessed his last air fight. First he shot down a Frenchman in the midst of a hostile squadron. Then he evidently had a jam in his machine gun and wanted to return to the air above our lines. A whole swarm of Frenchmen were on him. With a bullet through his head, he fell from an altitude of 9,000 ft – a beautiful death. Today I am going to fly at his funeral.

May 3 1916

to see anything. The trouble was that I had to go over the Moselle Mountains, straight through the valleys where the thunderstorm was raging. I got closer and closer to the black clouds which reached down to the earth. I flew as low as possible. I no longer knew where I was. The storm seized my plane as if it were a mere piece of paper and tossed it around.

"*All around me it was black. Beneath me the trees bent under the storm. Suddenly, a wooded height apeared before me. I had to go over it, and as luck would have it, my good Albatros got me over. I could only fly straight ahead, taking every obstacle that came along in turn. It was like riding a steeplechase over trees, villages, church towers, and chimneys. Lightning flashed all around me. At the time I did not know that lightning cannot strike a plane* (sic!).

"*I believed that death could come at any moment, for surely the storm would throw me into a village or forest. Then suddenly I saw a patch of light in front of me. The storm had already passed there; if I could reach this point, I would be saved. Gathering all my energy, as only a daring man can, I steered toward the light. Suddenly, as if wrenched out, I was free of the thunderclouds. I flew through streaming rain, but otherwise I was out of danger.* **"**

"*What did you say about Immelmann's death? In time, death comes to us all – also to Boelcke. The leader of Lothar's fighting squadron also did not return from the bombing flight. The day before, the leader of my old fighting squadron No.1 was also shot down. He was Baron von Gerstoff, one of the most efficient squadron leaders. I liked him very much.* **"**

June 22 1916

Relief from the lumbering biplanes came in the form of a part share in a Fokker monoplane with a Lt. Reimann. What it really amounted to was an opportunity to fly a rare monoplane, too few of which were available for the pilots that could possibly use them. Only the leading German aces like Oswald Boelcke and Max Immelmann, who were neck and neck with fourteen victories apiece, were permitted their own Fokker monoplanes. Manfred would fly the shared Fokker in the mornings and Reimann during the afternoons. It was Manfred's first experience with a monoplane and he recalled how strange it seemed to fly so small an aeroplane, one with a rotary engine. They could be tricky to handle, especially when taking off or landing.

Neither von Richthofen nor Reimann achieved success with the Fokker, each fearing the other would smash it up by accident, and the unhappy teaming ended when Reimann crashed the monoplane in no-man's land. That left Manfred sole user of another monoplane which stalled on his third flight in the type, causing it to crash without injury to the hapless occupant. It was evident that von Richthofen was a poor pilot and had to work hard to get the best out of the machines he flew. Flying is an expression of a pilot's personality and the freedom to exploit individual skills and innovative tactics is the benchmark of a 'fighter' pilot.

Man must meld with machine to achieve the definitive relationship between any particular pilot and a fighting flying machine. Manfred lacked that natural ability to fuse his sensory reactions into the control mechanisms of the aircraft he flew, relying instead on clearly planned, albeit logical, hunting skills tinged with cunning and extreme tenacity. But he was not a good pilot and his potential would not emerge clearly until he had the right kind of aeroplane to suit his special capabilities.

First steps in that direction came from an unexpected move when Kampfgeschwader Nr. 2 was ordered back to the Eastern Front flying bombing raids against the Russians. The unit would eventually be re-named Bombengeschwader Nr. 2 but by that time von Richthofen had left for more adventurous skies. His move came when Oswald Boelcke on a tour of the Eastern Front selected Manfred as a pilot for his new Jagdstaffeln, fighter squadrons then being formed on the Western Front with the specific purpose of searching for enemy aircraft. Now he had the chance he had waited months to be given. The chance to fly a single seater whose only purpose was to search out and destroy other aeroplanes in the sky.

Boelcke remembered having met von Richthofen on a train ten months earlier and saw in his spirited enthusiasm the essential skills needed to press home an air kill and return alive. Boelcke did not want good pilots. He wanted potentially good fighter pilots. He had his own ideas about tactics and the use of assembled air power in the skies over the battle front and von Richthofen seemed to fit the bill. It was at Boelcke's instigation that the Jagdstaffeln had been formed and now the theory behind their establishment could be applied to practical air fighting with honed pilots flying in formations of attacking aircraft.

The Eastern Front had been a spirited experience for von Richthofen. For several months he had flown bombers against massed troop formations and supply dumps, ammunition stores and railheads. With very little opposition in the air it had been carnage on the ground as successive bomb loads rained down, transforming the ground into a pummelled mass of torn and twisted iron, of spent shrapnel and blasted buildings. Von Richthofen claimed a vicarious thrill from this: **_I liked dropping bombs. Gradually my observer got the knack of flying perpendicular to the target and, with the help of an aiming telescope, he waited for the right moment to lay his eggs._**

It was particularly amusing to pepper the gentlemen down below with machine guns. Half-savage tribes from Asia (Russians – ed.) are much more startled when fired upon from above than are educated Englishmen. It is particularly interesting and comical to shoot at hostile cavalry. An aerial attack upsets them completely. Suddenly, all of them rush away in all directions of the compass. I should not like to be the commander of a squadron of Cossacks which has been fired upon with machine guns from aeroplanes.

Spring 1916

On several occasions, von Richthofen would seek out columns of cavalry or marching soldiers and swoop down with guns blazing to scatter them from roads and trackways. *It is particularly interesting and comical to shoot at hostile cavalry. An aerial attack upsets them completely. Suddenly, all of them rush away in all directions of the compass. I should not like to be the commander of a squadron of Cossacks which has been fired upon with machine-guns from aeroplanes.* And he should know what it would feel like, this ex-Uhlan from two war fronts who had forsaken the limitations of land warfare to take to the skies in combat.

We lined up at the firing range and fired our machine guns one after another down the line. The day before we had received our new planes, and the next morning Boelcke was to fly with us. We were all beginners; none of us had previously been credited with a success. Whatever Boelcke told us was taken as gospel. We knew that in the last few days he had shot down at least one Englishman a day, and many times two in a single morning.

September 1916

Manfred always remembered that day in August 1916, when he was asked to join Oswald Boelcke. *I heard a knock on my door early in the morning, and there he stood, a big man wearing the Pour le Merite, Germany's highest award. I didn't know what to say. I didn't dare think that he might have selected me to be one of his pupils. I almost hugged him when he asked me if I wanted to go with him to the Somme. Three days later I was on the train travelling across Germany to my new field. My ardent wish was fulfilled, and the most wonderful time of my life had begun.*

CHAPTER THREE *First Kills*

In name only, Manfred von Richthofen became a fighter pilot when he reported for duty on September 1, 1916, at Bertincourt near Cambrai where Jagdstaffel 2 had its airfield. Vizefeldwebel Reimann arrived with the unit's first aircraft, an Albatros D.I from Jasta 1. Essentially the equivalent of a British Royal Flying Corps Squadron, a German Jagdstaffel was smaller, with just 18 pilots and a total complement of 130 officers and men. The first Jagdstaffel had been formed on August 23 but the build-up of these elite fighter units was slow. Nevertheless, pilots came from both fronts to join them, several chosen by Boelcke himself.

When Jasta 2 formed on August 27 it had only three officers - Lts. Boelcke, von Arnim and Guenther - and 64 NCOs and men, but von Arnim was killed the following day. A day after that, Lt. Hoehne reported for duty and von Richthofen and Reimann were joined by Lts. Viehwager and Boehme on September 8. These were the first seven pilots of Jasgdstaffel 2 although for a time the unit would have a mixed bag of aircraft. The air war was changing. Max Immelmann had been killed during June after scoring a total of fifteen victories, the Fokker monoplanes no longer counted, and Allied pilots were fighting back using new aircraft and improved tactics. What little advantage the monoplanes had, they lost when increasing numbers of enemy aircraft were equipped with forward firing guns and equal performance.

Boelcke himself collected a Fokker D.III biplane from the Army aircraft park and with this aircraft (serial number 352/16) shot down his twentieth victim the following day. There was to be no respite in the search for enemy aircraft and Boelcke's energy went into leading his men by example and tuition. What better standard to set than maintaining a steady victory score. As Germany's leading ace, he was an example for all to follow and although very different in personality, Manfred von Richthofen idolised the Saxon with whom he had come to fly and to fight.

"At that time, I did not have the conviction, as I later had in similar cases – the conviction best described by the sentence 'He must fall.' In this, my first encounter, I was curious to see if he would fall. When one has shot down the first, second, or third opponent, then one begins to find out how the trick is done."

September 1916

During the first two weeks of September, Jasta 2's aircraft arrived slowly, some flown from production centres in Germany by officer pilots sent to fetch them from the factories. During this period, Boelcke increased his personal victory score to twenty-five and tutored his pupils in the art of formation flying and group attacks, showing by example in real combat the manoeuvres he intended his neophytes to copy. One year older than von Richthofen, Boelcke was also born under the constellation Taurus (only one week separated their birthdays) but the two were as different as could be imagined. Universally regarded as a great team leader, Boelcke put his men first and spent endless hours nurturing their clumsy techniques, honing and moulding them into disciplined air fighters.

Much nonsense has been made of the similarity between air warriors of World War I and knights of the Middle Ages. It is unlikely that those knights were possessed of the chivalry with which romantics have imbued them, and any similarity between the attitude of first war fighter pilots and that mythical behaviour is equally false. In each case these were professional men of war, equipped and trained to carry out a job for their country or their cause with the greatest chance of surviving to fight another day. Nevertheless, flyers of all nationalities had a high regard for each other, and once the business of combat was concluded many pilots and observers found themselves entertained by their captors until they were sent off to prison camps.

So it was to these parallel principles of allegiance to Kaiser and country and respect for the bravery of the enemy that the young pilots of Jasta 2 were introduced by the fatherly figure of Oswald Boelcke. They would each interpret those principles in their own way but none would forget the lessons or the counselling.

Below
September 1916. The first Albatros D.I scouts arrive at Jagdstaffel 2. Note the large white square behind the national markings, changed later to a white trim closely following the contours of the black cross.

The first opportunities to put these dictats into practice came along with a few Albatros D.II biplanes on Saturday, September 16. Now, at last, they had the mounts to carry them into battle with more than a fair chance of overwhelming the enemy. For these were not the Albatros biplanes von Richthofen had flown so many months before. They were, in their way, the tools through which Germany would restore the balance of power over the Western Front.

Agile, powerful, and with two forward firing machine guns, the Albatros D.II could reach 10,000 feet in less than fourteen minutes, half the time taken by the Fokker monoplanes. Speed and a rapid climb rate was very important where quick reaction to reported sightings of enemy aircraft in the air made a big

difference. In fifteen minutes an observation aircraft sighted from the ground would have flown a distance of more than twenty miles, probably in the opposite direction to the fighters climbing to attack. But outright performance was second to agility and manoeuvrability when it came to a close dog-fight, so one design advantage could not be compromised at the expense of the other. So it was that von Richthofen began his air fighting career on a type that was to remain his most familiar mount during the next year.

Most of his 80 victories would be scored in aircraft designed by Albatros. With two unconfirmed victories already, von Richthofen began his first official score card on September 17, the day Boelcke's fledglings took to the air as a group for the first time. It was a bright day with clear visibility and as the swarm of biplanes bounced along the grass and into the air optimism was high that success would favour the brave. Adhering to strict rules dictated by Boelcke, the formation grouped into a giant V as they sped off after a formation of eight B.E.2Cs from No. 12 Sqdn, RFC, protected by six F.E.2bs of No. 11 Sqdn, RFC.

Gaining first height and then the advantage of the glaring sun, Boelcke's fledglings positioned themselves above the British bombers and the escorting two-seaters. Diving to the attack from out of the sun, each man singled out a separate enemy aircraft. Von Richthofen went for an F.E.2b piloted by 2nd/Lt. L. B. F. Morris. It bore the serial number 7018 and carried Lt. T. Rees in the front cockpit as observer and gunner. Built by Boulton & Paul of Norwich, England, this particular aircraft was one of a batch of 100 ordered for the Royal Flying Corps. Although the biplane was a pusher, with the engine at the back inside a set of tail booms, firing at the ungainly looking contraption from behind was no safe haven. The observer could stand up in his front cockpit and fire above and to the rear.

Nevertheless, following advice from Boelcke, von Richthofen approached as close as he dare before opening fire but because he was diving to the attack he was above and behind the biplane. Rees stood up and fired at him while Morris flicked the controls first left, then right, to give his observer a clearer field of fire. Manfred broke off, dived into a cloud and came back below and behind the British aircraft, riddling it with bullets from so close a range he almost collided with the pitching underside. Both men were mortally wounded although Morris was able to get the aircraft down to a controlled crash landing. He died on his way to hospital. Von Richthofen's first combat report read as follows:

66 Dear Mamma:

You will have wondered at my continued silence, but this is the first chance I have had to sit down and take up a pen. I have been busy constantly of late. I had to fly a reserve plane with which I could not do much, being beaten in most encounters; but yesterday my new plane arrived and, just think, when I was giving it a try out, I sighted an English squadron right over our lines. Making for them, I shot one down. Its occupants were an English officer and a petty officer. I was rather proud of my attempt. Naturally, I have been credited with the downed plane. Boelcke is a mystery to everybody. Almost every flight sees him bring down an enemy. I was with him when he accounted for his twenty-fourth, twenty-fifth, twenty-sixth, and twenty-seventh, and took part in the fight.99

September 1916

Sept 17. 1916
Vickers No. 7018 Motor No. 701 Machine Guns
Nos. 17314,10372
Nr Villers Plouich 11 am

When patrol flying I detected shrapnel clouds in the direction of Cambrai. I hurried forth and met a squadron which I attacked shortly after 11 am. I singled out the last machine and fired several times at close range (10 metres). Suddenly the enemy propeller stood still. The machine went down gliding and I followed until I had killed the observer who had not stopped shooting until the last moment. My opponent went downwards in sharp curves. At approx. 1,200 metres a second German machine came along and attacked my victim right down to the ground and then landed next to the English plane.

Frhr. v.Richthofen.
Lieut.

Others did well that day and Boelcke got his 27th victim while Boehme joined von Richthofen in scoring his first official victory. Lt. Hoehne had shown the mettle of the new Albatros biplanes by bringing down his first victim the preceding evening only hours after they arrived at the airfield. Now Jagdstaffel 2 were to use the new fighting machines to good effect. But first, celebrations and congratulations made for a spirited evening. Boelcke was to give his pupils tankards to mark their first victories, an idea which appealed to Manfred's appetite for trophies. Soon, a Berlin jeweller received an order from Lt. von Richthofen for a single silver cup 5 cm high and 3 cm in diameter at the lip inscribed with a single line: 1 Vickers 2 17.9.16. the '1' denoted the first victory and the '2' stood for two-seater. It was Manfred's intention to order a single cup of this size for each successive victory.

Just six days later the Berlin jeweller was assured a second commission when von Richthofen gained another confirmed victory, this time over a single-seat reconnaissance and bomber type, the Martinsyde G.100 Elephant flown by Sgt. H. Bellerby of No. 27 Sqdn, RFC. Von Richthofen used only 300 shots to kill the pilot and bring the machine down near the Bapaume-Cambrai road during the late morning of September 23. He had the two Lewis guns retrieved and delivered to his airfield and was mistaken in reporting the aircraft's serial number as G.W.174, which was probably a part number from the Grahame-White company. Von Richthofen's third victim came seven days after the Martinsyde:

❝ *The battle on the Somme is not quite what you at home think it to be. For four weeks the enemy has been attacking us with superior forces, most notably artillery. And there are always fresh troops thrown into the battle. Our men fight excellently.*

During the next few days we will probably move our hangars further back. The whole looks very much like an open battle. I suppose you know that my friend Schweinichen has been killed. I had just made up my mind to visit him because he was stationed near by. That same day they got him. **❞**

September 1916

Sept 30. 1916

11.50 am

Near Lagnicourt

About 11.50 am. Accompanied by four planes of our Staffel, at 3,000 metres above our airfield at Lagnicourt, I attacked a Vickers squadron. I singled out an enemy machine and fired some 200 shots. It began gliding down in the direction of Cambrai. Finally it began to turn in crcles. The shooting had stopped and I saw that the machine was flying uncontrolled. As we were already rather far away from our front lines I left the damaged plane and selected a new adversary. Later on I could observe how the above mentioned machine, pursued by German Albatros machines, dashed burning to the ground near Fremicourt, the machine burnt to ashes.

Frhr. v. Richthofen.

Lieut.

Below

Then the leading German air ace, Oswald Boelcke, chats with Lt. Hoehne seated in the cockpit of a D.H.2 from No. 24 Sqdn, RFC, which he had shot down as his 24th victory. Manfred von Richthofen looks on.

With Lt. E. C. Lansdale and Sgt. Clarkson on board, this F.E.2b was the first of many aircraft von Richthofen would send to the ground in flames although there is some evidence to

suggest that the aircraft was set alight by the other Albatros scouts mentioned in the combat report. The sight of his flaming victim plunging to earth certainly made an impression upon the young man as he remarked in a letter to his mother almost a week later that it set his heart *'beating a bit more quickly'*. Von Richthofen was evidently mindful of the danger he faced. Five out of Jasta 2's ten pilots had been killed and within a few months others had suffered psychological breakdowns. Yet Manfred was ever eager to set out in search of prey and, already developing a taste for combat, exhibited none of the tensions he was to feel a year later.

Von Richthofen's fourth victory was scored on October 7 over a B.E.12, a type which first appeared on the Western Front in early August, ill equipped for its role as a fighting machine and destined as fighter fodder. For an expenditure of 400 rounds, the single-seat B.E.12 was downed near Rancourt, its pilot 2nd/ Lt. Fenwick shot through the head from close range. Von Richthofen reported that the type was new and had not been seen before. This was not strictly true and merely recorded von Richthofen's first encounter with the type. But success did not quell the urge to hunt and three days later Manfred submitted his fifth claim:

Oct 10. 1916

6 pm.

Boeux near Arras.

About 6 pm. I attacked a Vickers squadron at 3,500 metres, six kilometres to the east of Arras above Boeux. After having singled out a Vickers at whom I fired 300 shots, the enemy plane began to smoke and then started diving, steeper and steeper. I followed always shooting. The aircraft's propeller was only just turning and clouds of smoke were coming from the engine. The observer did not shoot at my machine any more. At this moment I am attacked from behind. It was ascertained after that the aircraft crashed to the ground and the pilot killed.

Frhr. v. Richthofen.
Lieut.

The fog of war has prevented identification of the aircraft and, consequently, its crew. If it was a single-seat B.E.12, why did von Richthofen mention an observer? Was he confused by the rear-facing Lewis gun that the pilot could operate as well as another Lewis above the upper wing? Probably not, for von Richthofen prided himself on getting in as close as possible to the enemy aircraft, ensuring a direct hit at some vulnerable spot, and he would surely have seen the observer. Yet mistaken

" *Dear Mamma:*

On September 30th, I brought down my third British plane. It was burned when he crashed to the ground. One's heart is beating a bit more quickly when the adversary whose face one has just seen goes down enveloped in flames from an altitude of 12,000 ft. Naturally, nothing was left either of the pilot or his plane when they crashed. I picked up a small plate as a souvenir. From my second, I have kept the machine gun, the breech-block of which had been jammed by a bullet. The Frenchman I brought down before Verdun is not on my record, as unfortunately we forgot to report him to headquarters. Formerly a pilot was decorated with the order Pour le Merite after he had brought down his eighth plane. Now they have discontinued that practice, although it becomes ever more difficult to shoot one down. During the last four weeks since the formation of the Boelcke squadron, we have lost five planes out of ten. **"**

October 5 1916

identity did occur when he claimed to have shot down a B.E.2 on October 25 while the aircraft in question was in fact a B.E.12. Perhaps the aircraft claimed on October 10 was a two-seat B.E.2, for the two could easily be confused in the heat of combat where attention focused on bringing the aircraft down and not on design characteristics.

Six days later, in worsening weather over the entire Front, von Richthofen scored another victory, confirmed later as his sixth. This time it definitely was a B.E.12, bearing the serial 6580 and flown by Lt. Tidsdale of the RFC. But his seventh claim on October 25 was contended by several counter claims from fellow officers for the same kill. Von Richthofen claimed that he was responsible for shooting down a two-seat B.E.2 (in fact, a B.E.12) from No. 21 Sqdn, RFC, bearing the serial 6629 and flown by Lt. A. J. Fisher. The last sentences of his filed combat report leaves no doubt about his feelings regarding the other claimants.

Oct. 25. 1916
9.35 am near Bapaume.
BE Two-seater

About 9 am. I attacked an enemy plane above the trenches near Lesboeufs. There was an unbroken cover of clouds at 2,000 metres altitude. The aircraft came from the German side and was just approaching our lines. I attacked and after 200 shots he went down in large circles and was forced back by the strong wind to the south of Bapaume. Finally the machine crashed to the ground. The plane was a BE, No 6629. The engine dashed into the earth, therefore number not legible. Pilot, a lieut, seriously wounded by shot in the bowels. Aircraft itself cannot be brought back, as under heavy fire. When I first saw the enemy plane there was no other German machine in the neighbourhood, and also during the fight no machine approached the scene of the action. As the enemy plane started to go down, I saw a Rumpler and several Halberstadter planes. One of these came down to the ground. It was piloted by Sgt. Major Mueller of Jagdstaffel 5. He claims to have fired first at 300 metres and then at 1,000 metres distance, some 500 shots at the enemy plane. Aterwards his gun jammed and the gunsight was blown away. Quite apart from these curious circumstances, a child knows that one cannot hit a plane from such ridiculous distances. Later, a second plane, a Rumpler, came down also claiming his share of the loot. But all the other planes in the area were perfectly sure that he had not taken part in the fight.

Frhr. v. Richthofen.
Lieut.

Manfred was furious that his claim should be contested when he was absolutely sure that no one could seriously question his right to credit for the B.E.12. It was typical of a dogmatism that would not endear him to fellow pilots in the way Boelcke was loved by his men. Von Richthofen believed that if he was convinced of a kill then the authorities should recognise in him a degree of integrity that was perhaps lacking in other officers. That this assumption was a flaw at all is a product of naivety rather than blatant arrogance although many would come to think of von Richthofen as rather too self-assured when making claims and combat statements.

In accounts of heady victories regularly logged against enemy aircraft it is too easy to forget the intensity of patrol schedules and the pressures on the pilots. For every flight that achieved a victory there were many more conducted without result. All this took its toll and eager young pilots vied with each other for scores and fame. As it was, the multiple claims for his B.E.12 deterred the Staff from assigning the victory of October 25 to von Richthofen and it has since become known as claim 6A, one of several doubtful actions. From the evidence, however, there is a strong probability that von Richthofen was the victor. Lt. Fisher's fate is unknown, although his wounds were said to be terrible indeed.

Next day, October 26, Oswald Boelcke scored his 40th and last victory in the air. Two days later he was dead. While chasing a British aircraft with Erwin Boehme, Boelcke was forced to take violent action to avoid colliding with another British aircraft pursued by von Richthofen. The undercarriage of Boehme's Albatros ripped the upper wing of Boelcke's biplane and he fell away out of control. Boelcke was Germany's first aerial tactician and, if measured by the effect he had on the development of aerial fighting and the men around him, he was the greatest leader of all the German aces during World War I. Manfred was moved to express his own feelings quite simply: **We always felt secure when he was along. There was only one Boelcke.**

Von Richthofen carried Boelcke's orders on a cushion before the black draped gun carriage drawn by six black horses at the funeral service in Cambrai. Reading from the First Book of Maccabees, an army chaplain offered up the words, "If our time has come, so let us die in knightly fashion for the sake of our brethren and not let our honour be shamed." After a salute fired by guards fresh from the trenches, the coffin was moved out of the cathedral to begin its journey to Dessau where the body was buried. A lone aircraft dropped a message in an envelope

It is a strange thing that everybody who met Boelcke imagined that he alone was his true friend. I have met about forty men, each of whom imagined that he alone had Boelcke's affection. Men whose names were unknown to Boelcke believed that he was particularly fond of them.

This is a curious phenomenon which I have never noticed in anyone else. Boelcke had not a personal enemy. He was equally pleasant to everybody, making no differences. His death shocked us.

1916

Dear Mamma:

Unfortunately, I missed the train to Boelcke's funeral, to which I was detailed as the representative of the squadron. Now I can only visit you at the middle of the month. Boelcke's death came about in the following manner: Boelcke, some men of our squadron, and myself were engaged in a battle with English planes. Suddenly, I see how Boelcke, while attacking his enemy, is rammed by one of our gentlemen, to whom, poor fellow, nothing else has happened. I followed him immediately. But then one of his wings broke away and he crashed down. His head was smashed by the impact: death was instantaneous. We are deeply affected, as if we had lost a favourite brother. During the funeral services and in the procession, I carried a pillow displaying his decorations. The funeral was like that of a reigning prince. In the last six weeks we have had out of twelve pilots six dead and one wounded, while two have suffered a complete nervous collapse. Yesterday I brought down my seventh shortly after I had accounted for my sixth. The ill luck of all the others has not yet affected my nerves.

November 3 1916

adressed "To the German Flying Corps." Inside it was a note: "To the memory of Captain Boelcke, our brave and chivalrous opponent. From, the English Royal Flying Corps."

Lt. Stephan Kirmaier took command of Jagdstaffel 2 until he too was killed a month later. Kirmaier scored a total of 11 victories before his death and Hauptmann Walz replaced him as head of the elite fighting unit until he too was replaced by Erwin Boehme in August 1917. By that time, von Richthofen had moved from Jasta 2 and become Germany's leading, and most famous, air ace. A new urgency possessed the fighter pilots of the German Air Service. The war in the air was becoming more violent, the pickings were getting less easy to knock down and the pressure of sustained combat was taking its toll of lives and nerves. Urged on by ambition and an increasing love of the hunt, the chase and the kill, von Richthofen was driven to succeed as none before him. The Berlin jeweller would be busy for a while longer.

Below
Von Richthofen carries Boelcke's medals and decorations on a black cushion at his memorial service in Cambrai cathedral during the afternoon of October 31, 1916.

CHAPTER FOUR *Ace Of Aces*

November 1916 brought Manfred five victories, raising his official score to 11. For his seventh accredited victory, von Richthofen fired 400 rounds into a F.E.2b flown by Sgt. G. C. Baldwin and 2nd/Lt. C. A. Bentham on November 3. Bearing the serial number 7010, the aircraft was flying low and von Richthofen attacked from a height of 1,800 metres in the presence of two other machines. Rarely did Manfred go hunting alone. His score was important and German records needed witnesses, preferably a piece of the claimed aircraft, before the kill could be officially credited. It was impossible in the case of this claim; the area was under fire and nothing could be retrieved.

Number eight was achieved six days later. Victory came about 10.30 am when von Richthofen attacked B.E.2c serial number 2506 flown by 2nd/Lt. J. G. Cameron and Lt.G. F. Knight as observer. The aircraft was one of a formation flying at 2,500 metres when it was attacked. He noted how they circled each other before the B.E.2c fell to earth, its pilot very seriously injured, the observer wounded in the shoulder. This victory should have given von Richthofen, the trophy hunter, cause for very great celebration indeed. Earlier in the war, a credited victory score of eight kills meant automatic award of the coveted Pour le Merite, or Blue Max. But no longer. The intensity of aerial fighting and the increased number of airmen now thought likely to exceed eight victories brought a change in that rule.

Nevertheless, the General Staff was keen to perpetuate the immortalisation of successful fighting airmen. They had already lost Immelmann, who despite his 15 victories was a brilliant pilot but a terrible shot, which was why some said he shot down as few as he did. And now Boelcke, with 40 victories, had been killed. Only a few pilots showed promise of achieving even greater laurels and von Richthofen was already singled out as a potential candidate. So, to encourage him to further successes, and compensate for not getting the Pour le Merite, von Richthofen was cited for The Order of the House of Hohenzollern.

Von Richthofen gained more than another victory in shooting down the B.E.2c on November 9. After landing, Manfred and Lt. Hans Imelmann, already credited with five victories, drove over to the scene of the wrecked aircraft each pilot had destroyed. Struggling through mud in the humid weather, their tunics unbuttoned and collars loosened, the two young airmen were confronted by the immaculate uniforms of senior German Army officers – and aristocrats to boot! Hearing first hand how the two Jasta 2 pilots had prevented at least two British bombers from attacking his headquarters, His Royal Highness the Grand Duke of Saxe-Coburg Gotha sent a message that evening to say he had enjoyed hearing the account and had awarded von Richthofen his special Medal for Bravery.

By now the weather had worsened and despite a concerted effort the Jasta was unable to achieve any measured success. Winter months were frequently like this and long periods could elapse between successful combats. Von Richthofen tried hard to find a victim and frustration followed boredom as for several days the flyers were unable to get off the ground due to squalls. Then, on November 20, the impasse broke. With three other pilots from Jasta 2 out for a morning patrol, von Richthofen pursued a flight of B.E.12s and attacked one of them at 9:40 am from 1,800 metres above Gueudecourt.

Chasing below cloud level and low down close to the ground, Manfred emptied 300 rounds at the fleeing biplane sending it to earth. During the afternoon von Richthofen shot down a two-seat F.E.2b which he reported as a **" Vickers Two Seater "**, another case of mistaken identity. It was at 4:15 pm over Gueudecourt that the aircraft fell to his guns and after reaching the ground was pummelled to destruction by artillery. This was frequently carried out by the home side, fearing that the wreckage might fall into enemy hands and deliver design secrets to the other side. The pilot, Lt. G. Doughty was killed but the observer, 2nd/Lt. G. Stall was alive although seriously wounded. He was taken prisoner and spent the rest of the war in Germany.

So far, von Richthofen had been lucky in his choice of target. He had only twice succeeded in shooting down two different types of single seater (B.E.12 and Martinsyde G.100) and they were hardly a match for the Albatros D.II with its twin Spandau machine guns. Not that this reflected a deliberate policy on his part to go for easy pickings. It was a fact of the first air war that the vast majority of aircraft caught in battle were either reconnaissance or spotter planes or bombers attacking ground targets. The single-seat 'fighter planes' had yet to emerge in force from the Allied side and there were few comparable types to the latest generation of German fighters.

All that was to change and von Richthofen came up against his first real adversary one November afternoon south of Bapaume. It was the day he tangled with one of the best loved British airmen of the time, Major Lanoe George Hawker of No. 24 Sqdn, RFC, described as the 'English Boelcke'. Major Hawker was the third British airman to receive the Victoria Cross and also sported the Distinguished Service Cross when he encountered von Richthofen. A man with an eye for technical detail and the inventor of several gadgets to aid the fighting flyer, Hawker gained his VC in August 1915, for an attack on three enemy aircraft simultaneously. He also introduced fur lined boots and came to be thought of as the flying man's aviator. He was the natural choice to command No. 24 Sqdn.

Flying D.H.2 pusher engined scouts, four pilots of 'A' Flight, No. 24 Sqdn, RFC, led by Capt. J. O. Andrews and including Maj. Hawker, set out on patrol early in the afternoon of November 23. Sighting five Albatros biplanes as they crossed the lines, Andrews signalled the attack but fearing they would be at a disadvantage because of their lower altitude, the German aircraft pulled away to gain height. As the British planes were drawn further across the German side of the lines, first one then another D.H.2 had to turn back with engine trouble. This left just Hawker and Andrews, who singled out an Albatros each and went in to the attack. Andrews' D.H.2 was hit, the engine misfired and its pilot had no option but to withdraw from the fray nursing a very sick aeroplane.

By chance the aircraft that Hawker attacked was the Albatros D.II flown by Manfred von Richthofen. The two were almost equally matched. Von Richthofen had ten confirmed victories to his credit - 11 if the disputed claim of October 25 is counted – while Hawker already had nine confirmed kills. Hawker was just sixteen months older than the German nobleman, who had yet to receive his country's highest award. It was to be one of von Richthofen's most challenging encounters, as he recalled later:

❝ It did not take long before (a British scout - ed.) dived for me, trying to catch me from behind. After a burst of five shots the cunning fellow had to stop, for I was already in a sharp left curve. The Englishman attempted to get behind me while I attempted to get behind him. So it went, both of us flying like madmen in a circle, with engines running full out at three thousand metre altitude. First left, then right, each intent on getting above and behind the other. I was soon acutely aware that I was not dealing with a beginner, for he did not dream of breaking off the fight. ❞

It was not easy to carry out these tight manoeuvres and maintain height so the conflict gradually descended to lower altitude, twisting and turning as each opponent fought for advantage. With only fixed, forward firing, machine guns to inflict damage the whole aircraft had to be pointed at the target. Round and round they went, each trying to get on the other's tail in so tight a circle that von Richthofen estimated they were only 250-300 feet apart. **❝ We went into circles again – fast and furious and as small as we could drive them. But always I kept above him and at times I could look down almost vertically into his cockpit and watch each movement of his head. If it had not been for his helmet and goggles, I could have seen what sort of face he had. ❞**

Down, down they went until the Englishman was in danger of not getting back to his lines. With a westerly wind facing him, Hawker would have to fight his way out from the German side at low altitude. There was a very real danger of being caught by ground fire and the advantage of height was a relative safety not easily given up. But that had been the price for this aerial tussle and Hawker made his move. Suddenly, he threw the D.H.2 into a succession of loops which brought him up and over toward von Richthofen's Albatros. In the fleeting seconds that the biplane came into view Hawker got off a burst of fire, the bullets whistling perilously close to von Richthofen.

Von Richthofen was never a superb pilot and frowned upon aerobatics, believing them to have no part in the serious business of aerial conflict. For him, the studied tactic of the stalking hunter and the kill cleanly executed by the skilled marksman was the way to defeat one's enemy. Now, Hawker was exhibiting skills Manfred could not match. He was close to being out-manoeuvred and in danger of succumbing to a chance

❝ Dear Mamma:

Accept my most sincere congratulations for your birthday. I trust this will be your last birthday in wartime. My eleventh Englishman was Major Hawker, twenty-six years old and commander of an English squadron. According to prisoners' accounts, he was the English Boelcke. He gave me the hardest fight I have experienced so far, until I finally succeeded in getting him down…Unhappily, we lost our commander three days ago, and eight days ago a plane of our squadron was brought down. ❞

November 25 1916

shot. Suddenly, Hawker flicked his biplane away and out of the fight. *We were getting so close to the ground that he would soon have to decide whether he would land behind our lines or would break the circle and try to get back to his own side.*

Von Richthofen continues the story of that epic chase: *The battle is now close to the ground. He is not a hundred yards above the earth. Our speed is terrific. He starts back for his front. He knows I am right behind him and close on his tail. He knows my gun barrel is trained on him. He starts to zigzag, making sudden darts right and left – left and right – confusing my aim and making it difficult for me to train my gun on him. But the moment is coming. I am fifty yards behind him. My machine gun is firing incessantly. We are hardly fifty yards above the ground – just skimming it.*

Hawker had very little ground to make up before crossing the lines and regaining the British side. Like other pilots von Richthofen was, theoretically, expected to remain on the German side of the lines for fear his aircraft would be captured or the pilot taken prisoner. *Now I am within thirty yards of him. He must fall. The gun pours out its stream of lead. Then it jams. Then it reopens fire. That jam almost saved his life. One bullet goes home. He is struck through the back of the head. His plane jumps and crashes down. It strikes the ground just as I swoop over. His machine gun rammed itself into the earth, and now it decorates the entrance over my door. He was a brave man, a sportsman and a fighter.*

Hawker had fallen just fifty yards before crossing the lines but it had been a hard fight and von Richthofen testified to his mother in a letter that, *He gave me the hardest fight I have experienced so far, until I finally succeeded in bringing him down.* As well as the Lewis gun, von Richthofen retrieved pieces of fabric from Hawker's machine bearing the serial number 5964. He had expended 900 rounds of ammunition during the long fight with the Englishman but his brief combat report failed to reflect how hard the fight had really been. Unlike many of his contemporaries, Manfred was not known for compiling wordy claim statements. He did, however, make sure that Lts. Wortmann and Collins were noted down as witnesses in case of any dispute!

More than two weeks passed before von Richthofen scored again, successfully forcing to the ground the second in a run of three D.H.2s he was to add to the mounting victory log for Jasta Boelcke. As his combat report for December 11 notes: *About 11.55, at an altitude of 2,800 metres, with Lt. Wortmann*

I must confess that it was a matter of great pride for me to learn that the Englishman I shot down on November 23 1916) was the English equivalent of our great Immelmann. Of course, I did not know who he was during the fight, but I did know from the masterly manner in which he handled his plane and the pluck with which he flew, that he was a wonderful fellow.

November 1916

Above

Pilots of Jasta 2, November 1916: (left to right) Lt. Sandel, Offstv. Max Mueller, Lt. von Richthofen, Lt. Guenther, Oblt. Kirmaier (who replaced Boelcke as Staffelfuehrer), Lt. Hans Imelmann, Lt. Koenig, Lt. Hoehne, Lt. Wortmann, Lt. Collin.

I attacked an enemy single seater squadron south of Arras (squad of 8 machines). I singled out one machine and after a short circling fight I damaged my adversary's engine and forced him to land behind our lines near Mercatel. The pilot was not seriously wounded. The pilot was, in fact, Lt. P. B. G. Hunt from No. 32 Sqdn, RFC, flying D.H.2 serial number 5986 with, as the meticulous German records show, engine number 30372. The third in his hat-trick of D.H.2s fell on December 20, a day in which von Richthofen shot down two aircraft bringing his confirmed score to 14. The scrap began when five Albatros of Jasta Boelcke attacked six D.H.2s of No. 29 Sqdn, RFC, quickly sending four of them spinning out of the fight, leaving one to be dealt with by von Richthofen and a second to escape. Lt. A. G. Knight was the unlucky pilot of D.H.2 number 7927, killed by von Richthofen at about 11:30 am above Monchy. As von Richthofen described for the administrative officer:

"*I attacked an enemy one-seater squadron at 3,000 metres above Monchy. After circling each other I managed to press my adversary down to 1,500 metres, where I attacked him at closest*

range (aircraft length). Immediately I saw that the enemy had been hit; first he went down in curves, then he dashed to the ground. The plane had only been attacked by me.»
Von Richthofen recovered the dead pilot's valuables, submitted them with the report, and kept the Lewis gun from the D.H.2 as a trophy.

The second aircraft that day was a F.E.2b from No. 18 Sqdn, RFC, piloted by Lt. L. G. D'Arcy with observer Sub/Lt. R. C. Whiteside, although von Richthofen was mistaken in thinking it to be yet another Vickers Two-Seater:

Jagdstaffel Boelcke
Dec. 20. 1916, 1:45 pm, above Noreuil
Vickers Two-Seater: A5446
Motor: Beardmore No 791.

Inmates: Pilot Lieut. L. G. D'Arcy, Observer unknown, had no identification disc. Inmates dead, plane smashed, one machine gun taken, valuables please find enclosed.
About 1.45 pm. With four planes of our Staffel I attacked an enemy squadron at 3,000 metres altitude above Noreuil. The English squad had thus far not been attacked by Germans and was flying somewhat apart. I had therefore an opportunity to attack the last machine. I was the foremost of our people and other German machines were not to be seen. After the first attack the enemy engine began to smoke; the observer had been wounded. The plane went down in large circles, I followed and fired at closest range. It was ascertained later on that I had killed the pilot. Finally the plane crashed to the ground. The plane is lying between Queant and Lagnicourt.

Frhr. v. Richthofen.
Lieut.

That von Richthofen was a disciplined fighter is evident from the rather bland descriptions in his combat reports. There were certain rules he scrupulously observed, most of which had been taught by Boelcke. He would never readily allow an adversary to gain the advantage of height in a dog-fight. Not for Manfred the wheeling and careening around a sky full of enemy planes searching for the lucky shot. To him, air combat was a science and had to be treated with calculated precision. Consequently, a favoured tactic was to keep his aircraft always slightly above and behind the enemy and never let the other fellow get into a similar position.

Equally important for von Richthofen was the determination to effect a coup de grace with certainty. He made a habit of getting very close to his opponent and opening fire only when he was

sure of hitting a vital part of the aircraft or the pilot himself.
Occasionally, this would bring grave risk of collision but
Manfred had the tenacity to stay right up with his victim until
the latter succumbed. Without doubt his sporting interests and
natural hunting instincts were a factor in giving him the edge
over many Allied pilots; but the comparison between boar
hunting and shooting down Englishmen in the air from a
bucking, wind tossed, aeroplane made of canvas and wood is
only superficial at best.

The third Christmas of the war came, and with it a chance to
meet with some of the family. Manfred's father, now mayor of a
German occupied town in France, paid a visit to Lagnicourt
where Jasta Boelcke were based. Lothar came along too and for
a while the father and his two eldest sons were able to enjoy
yuletide festivities. It was time for momentary reflection on the
fortunes a new year would bring. Lothar had joined the German
Air Service, serving first with Kampfstaffel Nr. 25 as an
observer before the mounting achievements of his brother
attracted him to become a pilot.

Having spent much time on numerous bombing raids the
younger von Richthofen was disillusioned with the tedium of
long flights in large aeroplanes whose sole duty was to fly as
straight and as level as possible to a distant target and back to
base. Yearning for adventure, Lothar requested a transfer from
the bombing unit to a flying training school and spent much of
the early winter in flying lessons. On Boxing Day he made his
first solo flight, as noted in a letter from Manfred to his mother:

On the Somme,
Dec. 28, 1916

Liebe Mamma:

*Papa and Lothar were with me on Christmas Day. It was a
memorable holiday. There is more fun to such a Christmas in the
field than you at home would think.*
*Our celebrations consisted of a Christmas tree and an excellent
dinner. On the next day, Lothar went up alone for the first time, an
event only equalled by his first victory.*
*Yesterday, I downed my fifteenth Englishman after I had shot my
second double two days before Christmas, Numbers 13 and 14.*

Manfred.

This reference to **" *two days before Christmas* "** must refer to the start of the festivities. The new year was to bring fame and a change of unit to the elder von Richthofen brother. Sometime before the old year ended Manfred began to plan for great achievements he felt destined to gain. He wanted to be recognised in the air as a special fighter, not merely one pilot of a German Jagdstaffel organised to harness the talents of several capable airmen. So to signal that self esteem and to mark upon his unit an intention to stand out both as an individual and as a von Richthofen, he chose to paint sections of his aircraft red. Uncertainty surrounds the reason for his choice of colour but it was most probably chosen because it represented the colours of his old Uhlan regiment.

CHAPTER FIVE *The Blue Max*

Manfred's fifteenth official victory had been scored two days after Christmas Day against a F.E.2b, serial number 6997, which once again was mistaken for a Vickers. This time he was flying Albatros D.II serial number 491/16 when the action took place at 4:25 pm. With just 300 rounds the British biplane went down out of control, pursued by von Richthofen to a height of 3,000 feet, to crash behind trenches near Ficheux. The names of the occupants are unrecorded and Manfred cited personnel from Air Batteries 13 and 47 as witnesses to the kill.

The sixteenth victory came four days into January 1917, and gave von Richthofen the first chance to sample a new threat to the Jagdstaffeln's Albatros scouts. The British had introduced a new scout biplane from Sopwith at the end of the summer. Called the Pup, it was one element in a shift of balance that would increasingly favour British and French air units in the months ahead. Suffering a terrible beating in the air during the

" My sixteenth foe had fallen. Consequently, I was the leading fighter pilot (living). This was the goal I wanted to achieve. A year ago, when we were in training, my friend Bodo von Lyncker asked me: "What is your goal? What would you like to achieve as a flyer?" In jest I had answered: "Well, it must be quite nice to be the leading fighter pilot." Neither I nor anyone else believed I should come to that. Boelcke, when asked, "Who looks as if he would be a good fighter pilot?" is supposed to have said – of course not to me personally but it was told to me later by another – "That is the man!" pointing his finger at me."

January 1917

Battle of the Somme which began in mid-1916, the British Royal
Flying Corps had been reinforced by elements of the Royal
Naval Air Service with aircraft of this type.

Since September, No. 8 (Naval) Sqdn, RNAS, had been
shooting down German aeroplanes over the Western Front with
Sopwith Pup scout biplanes. Sopwith aeroplanes had already
achieved respect with the 1 1/2 Strutter, many of which had
been diverted from the Naval Air Service to the Flying Corps to
consolidate the offensive over the Somme. But the Pup was
something different. Small, it had a wing span of only 26 ft 6 in,
the 100 hp Gnome powered Pup could reach a height of 10,000
feet in little more than twelve minutes. The Albatros D.II of
Jasta 2 was outclassed, as seen by von Richthofen when he went
to fight Sopwith Pup number N5193 from No. 8 (Naval) Sqdn,
RNAS, piloted by Flt/Lt. A. S. Todd:

Jagdstaffel Boelcke.
Jan. 4. 1917.
4.15 pm.
Near Metz au Couture.
Sopwith One Seater, No LRT 5193.
Motor: 80 hp Le Rhone No 5187.

*A new type of plane, never seen before, but as wings broken, badly
discernable.*

*Pilot: Lieut. Todd, killed, papers and valuables enclosed. About
4.15 pm. Just after starting, we saw above us at 4,000 metres
altitude four planes unmolested by our artillery. As the anti-aircraft
guns were not firing we took them for our own. Only when they
were nearer did we notice that they were English. One of the
English planes attacked us and we saw immediately that the enemy
plane was superior to ours. Only because we were three against one
did we detect the enemy's weak points. I managed to get behind him
and shoot him down. The plane broke up whilst falling.*

Frhr. v. Richthofen.
Lieut.

Doubtless, von Richtofen would have liked to have brought
down the Pup intact and presented it to the intelligence experts
for examination, thus gaining the credit for having delivered one
of the new machines for comparison with the Albatros. That
distinction, however, went to another German aviator on the day
Manfred got his sixteenth official victory. Lt. Friedrich
Mallinckrodt of Jagdstaffel 10 had the honour of delivering
Sopwith Pup A626 intact to the German side of the lines. It had
been delivered to France in November 1916, and arrived with

No. 8 (Naval) Sqdn, RNAS, before the end of the year, where it had served with 'B' Flight.

But Manfred need not have worried about impressing the General Staff for he received orders to leave Jasta Boelcke and command a fighting unit of his own - Jagdstaffel 11 at Douai. It was an honour indeed, but not the one he sought. He specifically wanted the Blue Max which he felt he had rightfully won. After all, had he not achieved twice the confirmed victory score which until recently would have automatically qualified him for the Pour le Merite? Others seemed to think so too because the notification that he had finally been awarded Germany's highest military medal came on January 16. Now he had joined the ranks of men like Boelcke. He had his own fighting unit and he had the Blue Max.

He now had to face some of the problems that go with leadership and for his role model it was natural he would fall back on his mentor, Oswald Boelcke, who had so inspired the new recruits to Jasta 2. He realised he needed to get to know his men, and motivation was sorely needed. Jasta 11 had been formed in September 1916, and in four months had failed to score a single victory. It had been easier for Boelcke, thought Manfred. He had no precedent against which to compare performance. Now he had to mould his new unit into an effective fighting machine, transforming each pilot into an efficient member of the team. That was difficult for von Richthofen, who did not see himself as a team leader.

Jasta 11 had twelve pilots when Manfred joined them. Some of them would achieve fame under von Richthofen's baton, especially Karl Allmenroeder and Kurt Wolff. Others would join later and rise to equal stardom. Manfred von Richthofen was already an impressive role model for the stagnating Jagdstaffel he had come to lead. Not only a prominent ace but a holder of the Pour le Merite as well. But first von Richthofen had to temper personal drive and enthusiasm for combat with a division of responsibility that gave equal time and effort to fashioning a new team of aggressive aerial combatants. Like his master before him, von Richthofen wanted to lead by example because he wanted his men to fight like he did. So, on January 23, he achieved the first victory for Jasta 11 and raised to seventeen his personal victory log:

Jan. 23rd. 1917
4.10 pm.
Trenches above Lens (to the south-west).

❝*One day a telegram came, which read: "Lt. von Richthofen designated to be leader of Jagdstaffel 11." I must say, I was more annoyed than pleased. I had become so thoroughly acquainted with my comrades in Jasta Boelcke that now to have to begin getting settled anew was irksome. Besides, I would rather have had the Pour le Merite.*

*Two days later – we were cozily sitting around at Jagdstaffel Boelcke and celebrating my leaving – a telegram from Headquarters came, saying that His Majesty was graciously presenting me with the Pour le Merite. Naturally, there was great joy all round. It was a mark of progress.***❞**

January 1917

❝*Dear Mamma:*

*I am certain you wonder at my silence. So much has happened in the meantime that I do not know where to start. I have been appointed commander of the Eleventh Combat Squadron stationed in Douai. I left the Boelcke squadron only very reluctantly. But no matter how hard I resisted I had to go. The Eleventh Squadron has been in existence as long as my former one, but so far it has no enemy to its credit and the way they do things here is not very edifying. I have twelve officers under my command. Luck has been with me. On the first time up with my new command, I brought down my seventeenth, and on the following day, number eighteen. As I settled down with the latter, one of my wings broke at an altitude of 900 feet, and it was nothing short of a miracle that I reached the ground without a mishap. On the same day the Boelcke squadron lost three planes, among them dear little Imelmann – a thousand pities. It is quite possible that they met with a similar accident. Unhappily, there is no chance of leave, and I would have liked to show you my Pour le Merite.***❞**

January 27 1917

No details of aircraft, plane dropped on the enemy's side. About 4.10 pm. With seven of my planes I attacked an enemy squadron west of Lens. The arcraft I had singled out caught fire after 150 shots, discharged from a distance of 50 metres. The plane fell, burning. The occupants of the plane fell out at a height of 500 metres. Immediately after the plane had crashed I could see a heavy black smoke cloud arising. The plane burnt for quite a while, flames frequently flaring.

Frhr. v. Richthofen.

The aircraft von Richthofen had brought down was a single-seat F.E.8 from No. 40 Sqdn, RFC, piloted by 2nd/Lt. J. Hay. The type was the first British fighter plane, developed at the Royal Aircraft Factory at Farnborough. A pusher, it bore a superficial resemblance to the D.H.2 and carried a single Lewis machine gun in front of the pilot. It was the only aircraft of this type the Baron would shoot down. It was followed a day later by his eighteenth victim, an F.E.2b from No. 25 Sqdn, RFC, flown by Capt. O. Grieg and Lt. J. E. MacLenan:

Jan. 24th. 1917 Occupants: Pilot - Capt. O. Grieg 12.15 pm.
Observer - Lt. MacLenan
West of Vimy.
Fixed motor.
Aircraft No 6937
Motor No 748.

At about 12.15 pm accompanied by Vfw. Howe I attacked the leading plane of an enemy formation. After a long fight I forced my adversary to land near Vimy. The inmates burnt the plane after landing. I myself had to land, as one wing had cracked at 300 metres. I was flying an Albatros D III.

According to the British inmates my red aircraft was not unknown to them as, when being asked who had brought them down, they answered 'le petit rouge'. Two machine guns were seized by my Staffel. It was not worthwhile salvaging the aircraft as it was completely burnt.

Frhr. v. Richthofen.

Von Richthofen was flying one of the very few new Albatros D.III biplane scouts which had appeared at the end of 1916 as replacements for the now obsolescent D.II. Boelcke had personally selected the Albatros for his then newly formed Jasta 2 and von Richthofen maintained the tradition largely because he was unfamiliar with alternative single-seat scouts. But during the fight with his eighteenth victim, he had been fired upon by

another F.E.2b and this had caused the observer of that aircraft, 2nd/Lt. A. C. Servers to claim von Richthofen as a victory score.

Whether von Richthofen's aircraft was struck by a lucky round from the F.E.2b or whether it suffered structural failure is unknown for certainty although the latter is most probable. But he did have cause to land, driving home a vulnerability he was increasingly prone to disregard. Elsewhere along the Western Front, two German pilots died for the Fatherland because the wings of their aircraft cracked in flight. One of them was the young Hans Imelmann who had so recently tramped a muddy field to meet the Grand Duke of Saxe-Coburg Gotha.

This reference to his red Albatros is the first mention of the feature that would characterise von Richthofen's aircraft until his death. There is, however, no evidence to suppose that he had the complete aircraft painted red. At first only the fuselage, wheel covers and possibly the struts were so brightly coloured. It represented a departure from official orders on aircraft markings that would have been impossible in the British air services. Yet it was of value to the German political machine because it provided a sign of boldness the public could identify

Above
Carrying the stick that will later become famous as the Geschwaderstock, Manfred poses in front of an Albatros D.II, with (left to right) Kirmaier, Imelmann and Wortmann.

with. The sheer audacity of advertising not only the presence of an enemy machine but the identity of the proud pilot too was a fillip to civilian morale as well as that of the German Air Service.

Manfred von Richthofen was certainly achieving recognition outside the tight band of pilots in Jasta 11, and the German propaganda machine was already at work advertising his successes. Postcards and newspaper reports were issued on all airmen of even modest achievement; in stark contrast to the British, where individual fame was frowned upon and positively discouraged, the Germans heaped laurels upon their young warriors. Letters began to arrive at his airfield from all over Germany, many from women who idolised the young flyers and singled out von Richthofen for his boyish good looks and warm, deep eyes.

Some of these letters were made the butt of humour and ribald merriment. Others were kept discreetly aside for personal reply. Yet Manfred did not easily assume the mantle of paramour as many of his brother officers did, nor did he court the favours of any one girl for a permanent relationship. Three days after his eighteenth victory, Manfred wrote home to his mother:

With the Eleventh Combat Squadron,
Jan. 27, 1917.

Dear Mamma:

I am certain you wonder at my silence. So much has happened in the meantime that I do not know where to start. I have been appointed commander of the Eleventh Combat Squadron stationed in Douai.
I left the Boelcke squadron only very reluctantly. But no matter how hard I resisted I had to go. The Eleventh Squadron has been in existence as long as my former one, but so far it has no enemy to its credit and the way they do things here is not very edifying. I have twelve officers under my command...
Unhappily, there is no chance of leave, and I would have liked to show you my Pour le Merite.

Manfred.

Flying a Halberstadt D.II instead of his usual mount, von Richthofen achieved the only official victory of his career not obtained on an Albatros or a Fokker when he shot down a B.E.2e of No. 16 Sqdn, RFC, on the first day of February 1917. The Halberstadt had been introduced to help supplement the Fokker D.II biplanes, in turn a replacement for the totally obsolescent Fokker monoplanes. With a top speed of only 90 mph, they had a nifty climb rate and could attain a height of 10,000 feet in 15 minutes. The type was, however, handicapped as a fighter by having only one machine gun, mounted to the port side of the fuselage. Despite this, von Richthofen scored again:

Feb. 1st. 1917.

BE Two-Seater.

4 pm.

Over trenches 1 kilometre south west of Thelus.

Occupants: Lieut. Murray and Lieut. McRae, both wounded and died on February 2nd.

Aircraft No 6742.

About 4 pm. Whilst flying with Lieut Allmenroeder at 1,800 metres altitude I spotted an artillery flyer (BE two-seater). I managed to approach to within 50 metres of him unnoticed, with my Halberstadter machine. From this distance I fired 150 shots until I was within one plane's length of him. The enemy plane then went down in large, uncontrolled, right hand spirals pursued by Allmenroeder and myself. The plane crashed into the barbed wire of our first lines. The occupants were both wounded and were made prisoners by the infantry. It is impossible to salvage the plane.

Frhr. v. Richthofen.

February 1917 was a bad month for flying and von Richthofen went two weeks without scoring a single victory. Then he made up for it by achieving two in one day. The first encounter took place when von Richthofen attacked a B.E.2d from No. 2 Sqdn, RFC, **66** *after flying back from a conference with Jagdstaffel Boelcke. I spotted an enemy artillery flyer at a height of 2,000 metres west of Loos. I attacked the enemy and approached unnoticed to 50 metres. After firing some several hundred shots the plane dashed to the ground falling into the trenches. The pilot (Lt. C. D. Bennet) was killed and the observer (2nd/Lt. H. A. Croft) seriously injured when landing.* **99** In fact, Croft was dead, and not Bennet, although it was two months before Bennet's parents received a message from the Red Cross on April 18 that he was alive and a prisoner of the Germans.

That was von Richthofen's 20th official victory but later that day, **66** *About 4.45 pm with five planes from my Staffel I attacked artillery flyers at a low altitude near Lens. Whilst my gentlemen attacked a second B.E., I attacked the one flying nearest to me. After the first hundred shots the observer ceased firing. The plane began to smoke and twisted down in uncontrolled spirals to the right. As this was not a conclusive end for me, especially over the*

66 The adversary often slips downward over one wing or lets himself fall like a dead leaf in order to shake off an attack. In order to stick to one adversary, one must on no account follow his tactics, as one has no control over the machine when falling like a dead leaf.

Should the adversary, however, attempt to evade attack by such tricks, one must dash down without losing sight of the enemy plane. When falling, like a dead leaf, or intentionally falling wing over wing, the best pilot loses control of his machine for a second or two, therefore it is a manoeuvre to be avoided.99

February 16 1917

66 Looping the loop is worse than worthless in air fighting. Each loop is a great mistake. If one has approached an adversary too close, a loop only offers a big advantage to the adversary. Change of speed should be relied upon to maintain the position desired, and this is best effected by giving more or less throttle.99

February 16 1917

*enemy's lines, **I continued shooting until the left part of the wing came off.***" The importance von Richthofen applied to the stringent rules of qualification for a certified victory comes through the language of the combat report.

He writes on: **"As the wind was blowing at a velocity of 20 metres a second, I had drifted far over the enemy's side. Therefore I could observe that the enemy plane touched the ground southwest of Mazingarbe. I could see a heavy cloud of smoke in the snow arising from where the plane was lying. As it was foggy and already rather dark I have not got any witnesses, from the air or on the ground.***"** Confirmation of this aerial duel was granted in the absence of witnesses because of reports from ground batteries that an aircraft was seen crashing far over the British side of the lines. There is no reason to doubt von Richthofen's claim but the fact that he was allowed to count it shows how well it suited the Army to have him increase his score.

During this period a concerted examination of the way the Jagdstaffeln operated brought the need for much administrative work to the practically minded Manfred. It was an opportune time for the Army to investigate the efficiency of the concept; the weather was appalling. They determined that a new alert system was needed to improve the efficiency with which scout units could be dispatched to attack approaching enemy aircraft. Men and material were in short supply and the General Staff wanted to make the optimum use of every aircraft delivered from the already overworked factories.

Von Richthofen was required to write reports on air combat and to summarise the techniques he used to achieve success. The formula for good results was elusive and relied more on individual tactics than a standard code to be taught and mastered. His superiors wanted the fruits of his knowledge and he was encouraged to write down his thoughts and ideas although in practice that merely codified von Richthofen's own prejudices. But soon the respite was over and there began the most intense period of successful aerial combat von Richthofen ever achieved.

"The best method of flying against the enemy is as follows: The officer commanding the group, no matter how large, should fly lowest, and should keep all machines under observation by turning and curving. No machine shoud be allowed either to advance or to keep back. More or less, the whole squadron should advance curving. Flying straight on above the front is dangerous, as even machines of the same type of plane develop different speeds. Surprises can be avoided only when flying in close order. The commanding officer is responsible that neither he nor any of his pilots are surprised by the enemy. If he cannot see to that, he is no good as a leader."
February 16 1917

CHAPTER SIX *The Supreme Victory*

In the two months of March and April 1917, Manfred von Richthofen was credited with shooting down a total of 31 aircraft. In a period of just 56 days he accounted for 55 airmen in eleven different types of aircraft flown by the Royal Flying Corps over the Western Front. These were grim days indeed. Whereas previous tactics had called for the German scouts to patrol behind the German lines, they were now required to fight up and down along the line of trenches. Of a total of 27 British aircraft shot down by the Germans during December 1916, 17 were brought down into the British lines and almost all aerial combat between scout aircraft took place right over the battle front.

With March came a major drive by the Germans in the Arras sector and a massive onslaught of air power pressed hard against squadrons of the Royal Flying Corps. It was into this maelstrom of furious activity that von Richthofen threw himself and Jasta 11, now in fierce competition with his former unit, Jasta Boelcke. German aircraft were sent out in groups of six or eight to harry the reconnaissance machines and disrupt aerial photography. During March, 120 British aircraft of the RFC were shot down, 59 of them on the British side of the lines. But the Germans were being pressed ever harder.

For the Battle of Arras that began with a British air offensive on April 4, the Royal Flying Corps had approximately 365 serviceable aircraft in 25 squadrons, of which about 130 were single-seaters facing 195 German aircraft of which less than 100 were fighting scouts. By April 9, between Lille and Peronne, the

66 The English single-seater pilots always fly in squad formation when on pursuit work. Reconnoitering and artillery fire is also now carried on by squads of two-seater machines. Many English airmen try to win advantages by flying tricks while engaged in fighting, but, as a rule, it is just these reckless and useless stunts that lead them to their deaths.

When flying in large squads, the English planes keep close together in order to be able to come to one another's assistance at any given moment. When attacked, they maintain even closer formation. If an English plane which has fallen behind is attacked, the first planes of the enemy formation make left and right turns and hurry to its assistance. After the rest of the formation has passed them, they close up the rear as the last planes.99

Spring 1917

Far Right
A gathering of Albatros D.III scouts at Roucourt near Douai with von Richthofen's machine second from front. Note the red painted fuselage and tail with just the black crosses remaining visible.

British had 754 aircraft facing 264 German aircraft. But of these totals the British had 385 fighting scouts to the Germans' 114. Outnumbered more than three to one, Jasta 11 was in the thick of the fray. It was a time for kill or be killed and the frantic cycle of patrols, repairs, re-fuelling, re-arming and more patrols was an almost ceaseless frenzy of activity.

The first three victims that fell to von Richthofen's guns during this intense period were shot down on March 3 and 4. Like his preceding victory of February 14, the one claimed on March 3 had no witnesses but von Richthofen received credit for it nevertheless: *Together with Lieut. Allmenroeder I attacked two enemy artillery flyers at a low altitude over the other side of the lines. The wings of the plane broke off that I attacked; it dashed down and broke up on the ground.* Described as a B.E.2c, it fell near Souchez around 5:00 pm.

Next day von Richthofen took off after the rest of Jasta 11, *and was looking for my squadron when I spotted a single BE. My first attack was apparently a failure as the enemy aircraft tried to escape by turning and diving. After having forced my adversary down from 2,800 to 1,200 metres, he imagined himself safe and flew in a straight line once again. I took advantage of this, got behind him and fired some 500 shots at him. He dived down, but in such a steep way that I could not follow. According to our infantry observation units the plane crashed to the ground in front of our trenches.*

This victory has a question mark hanging over it for the aircraft that was witnessed by German ground troops as it crashed to earth may not have been the one von Richthofen attacked around 12:50 pm. There was a bad ground mist that day and von Richthofen lost sight of his victim as he followed it down. The wreckage attributed to von Richthofen's victim belonged to a B.E.2d, serial number 6252, flown by F/Sgt. R. J. Moody and 2nd/Lt. E. E. Horn fron No. 8 Sqdn, RFC, both of whom were killed.

The time of the crash and the location of the wreckage does not coincide with von Richthofen's report. But they do tie up wth a claim by Werner Voss for his twelfth victory. It is likely that von Richthofen had attacked and pursued into cloud a B.E.2d (5785) flown by Sgt. J. E. Prance and Lt. J. B. E. Crosbee of No. 2 Sqdn, RFC, which recovered and flew home below the mist. From Jasta Boelcke, the 19 year old Voss was second to von Richthofen in victories and had shot down his first victim as recently as November 27, 1916.

About 4:20 that afternoon, **"Accompanied by five planes from my Staffel I attacked an enemy squadron above Acheville. The Sopwith I had singled out continued flying for quite a while under my fire. Whilst turning and after my 400th shot the plane lost a wing. Machine dashed downwards. It was not worth while salvaging the plane because parts were spread over Acheville and surroundings. Two machine guns were collected by my Staffel. "** The aircraft had been a Sopwith 1 1/2 Strutter flown by 19 year old Lts. H. J. Green and W. Reid from No. 43 Sqdn, RFC.

Five days later, von Richthofen scored his 25th official victory by attacking nine F.E.8s from No. 40 Sqdn, RFC. The five Albatros scouts had their work cut out and the fight lasted for more than thirty minutes before von Richthofen shot down a D.H.2, which may have joined the fray, for an expenditure of 100 rounds. It crashed just 500 yards on the German side of the lines. One of the F.E.8 pilots had a lucky escape while trying to make an emergency landing. His aircraft caught fire close to the ground but the pilot jumped out at the last minute and escaped with his life.

Once again, von Richthofen came close to death when bullets from an attacking aircraft punctured both fuel tanks and the engine. With a strong smell of leaking fuel spurting through the thin ruptured tanks, von Richthofen shut off the engine and glided down to about 1,000 ft, selected a patch of clear ground near Henin Lietard and landed. He had seen too many victims go down in flames to disregard the signs. Two days later he was victorious again when **"I had lost my squadron and was flying alone. I had been observing an enemy artillery flyer for some time. At a favourable moment I attacked the BE machine (B.E.2d serial number 6232 flown by 2nd/Lt. J. Smith and Lt. E. Byrne from No. 2 Sqdn, RFC,) and after 200 shots the body broke in half. The plane fell smoking into our lines. "** That was victory number 26. Six days later, another double:

Mar. 17. 1917
Vickers Two-Seater.
11.30 am.
Oppy
Occupants: Both killed, no identity discs, names found on maps were Smith and Heanley.
Aircraft No: A3439.
Engine No: 854.
Machine Guns: 19901 and 19633.

About 11.30 with nine of my machines I attacked an enemy squadron of 16 units. During the fight I managed to force a Vickers Two Seater aside and after 800 shots brought him down. Under my

"It became clear to me that I had been hit, or, rather, my machine had been hit. At the same time I noticed a fearful stench of petrol, and I saw that the motor was running slow. The Englishman noticed it too, for he started shooting with redoubled energy, while I had to stop.

I went right down. Instinctively I switched off the engine. I left in the air a thin white cloud of gas. I knew its meaning from previous experience with my enemies. Its appearance is the first sign of a coming explosion. I was at an altitude of 9,000 ft and had to travel a long distance to get down. By the kindness of Providence, my engine stopped running.

I have no idea with what rapidity I went downward. At any rate, the speed was so great that I could not put my head out of the machine without being pressed back by the rush of air. Soon, I had lost sight of the enemy plane...I had fallen to an altitude of perhaps 1,000 ft, and had to look out for a landing...

I found a meadow. It was not very large, but it would suffice if I used due caution. Besides, it was very favourably situated on the high road near Henin-Lietard. There I meant to land, and I did, without accident. "

March 1917

machine gun fire the plane lost its open work fuselage. The occupants were killed and were taken for burial by local Commanders at Oppy.

Frhr. v. Richthofen.

Mar. 17. 1917

BE Two-seater.

5pm.

Above trenches west of Vimy.

No details, as plane landed between lines.

I had spotted an enemy infantry flyer. Several attacks directed from above produced no results, especially as my adversary did not accept combat and was protected from above by other machines. Therefore I went down to 700 metres and attacked him from below; he was flying at 900 metres. After a short fight my opponent's aircraft lost both wings and fell. The machine crashed into no mans land and was fired at by our infantry.

Frhr. v. Richthofen.

The first was a F.E.2b flown by Lt. A. E. Boultbee and Air/Mech. F. King from No. 25 Sqdn, RFC. The maps bearing the names Smith and Heanley had been borrowed. The second was a B.E.2c from No. 16 Sqdn, RFC, with 2nd/Lt. G. M. Watt and Sgt. F. A. Howlett. In the morning engagement, von Richthofen had taken advantage of the new aircraft alert system which was proving distinctly effective at vectoring the scouts on to reported aircraft. Linked by telephone to the Jagdstaffeln they would alert, observers along the front lines would report sightings of enemy aircraft approaching and provide information on the size and makeup of the force.

❝ Baron Manfred von Richthofen

Sir: I witnessed on March 17, 1917, your air fight and took this photograph which I send to you with hearty congratulations, because you seldom have the occasion to see your prey. Here's to the next!

With fraternal greetings Baron von Riezenstein Colonel and Commander 87th Reserve Infantry Regiment.❞

March 1917

Mar. 21st. 1917.

BE Two-seater.

5.30 pm.

Hill 123, north of Neuville.

Aircraft details unknown, as plane came down on the enemy's side. Messages came through that enemy planes had been seen at 1,000 metres altitude in spite of bad weather and strong east winds. I went up by myself intending to bring down an infantry or artillery flyer.
After one hour I spotted at 800 metres a large number of enemy artillery flyers beyond the lines. They sometimes approached our front, but never passed it. After several vain attempts I managed, half hidden by clouds, to take one of these BE's by surprise and to attack him at 600 metres, 1 kilometre beyond our lines. The adversary made the mistake of flying in a straight line when he tried

to evade me and was thus just a second too long in my fire (50 shots). Suddenly he went into two uncontrolled circles and dashed, smoking, to the ground. The aircraft was completely ruined. It fell in section F.3.

Frhr. v. Richthofen.

The crew of this aircraft, a B.E.2c from No. 16 Sqdn, RFC, were Sgt. S. H. Quicke and 2nd/Lt. W. J. Lidsey. Von Richthofen's next victim, his 30th official kill, fell to his guns three days later wounding Lt. R. P. Baker and sending him into a prison camp for the duration of the war. He was flying a Spad S.7, the first French built aircraft for which von Richthofen received official credit, belonging to No. 19 Sqdn, RFC:

66 *Dear Mamma:*

Yesterday I brought down my thirty-first, and the day before my thirtieth. Three days ago I received my appointment as First Lieutenant, and thus gained a full half year. My squadron is shaping well. It really gives me great pleasure. Lothar had his first air encounter yesterday. He was satisfied with it because he touched his adversary who, in our parlance, 'stank,' leaving a black, smelly trail behind him. He did not come down, of course – that would have been too much luck. Lothar is very conscientious and will do well. How is Papa, and how did you like yesterday's official army report? **99**

March 26 1917

Mar. 24th. 1917.
11.55 am.
Givenchy.
Occupant: Lt. Baker.
Aircraft: A Spad with Hispano Engine. The first here encountered.
Plane No: 6706. (it was in fact A6706 - ed.)
Engine: Hispano-Suiza 140 HP.
Machine Gun No: Maxim 4810.

I was flying with several of my gentlemen when I observed an enemy squadron passing our front. Aside from this squadron two new one seaters, which I did not recognise, were flying. They were extremely fast and handy. I attacked one of them and ascertained that my machine was the better one. After a long fight I managed to hit my adversary's tank. The propeller stopped turning. The plane had to go down. As the fight had taken place over the trenches, my adversary tried to escape, but I managed to force him to land behind our lines near Givenchy. The plane turned upside down in a shell hole. The aircraft was captured by our troops.

Frhr. v. Richthofen.

Next day, von Richthofen shot down another French aircraft, flown by 2nd/Lt. C. G. Gilbert of No. 29 Sqdn, RFC, with the serial number A6689. **66** *An enemy squadron crossed our lines. I went up, overtaking their last machine. After only a few shots, the enemy's propeller stopped running. My adversary landed near Tilley, damaging his plane. I observed that some moments later the plane began to burn.* **99** No doubt set alight by the pilot, who survived the ordeal and was eventually taken to a prison camp.

Roused from his bed by an enthusiastic report that the English were coming, von Richthofen flew to his 32nd victory during the early morning on April 2: **66** *I attacked an enemy artillery* *flyer. After a long fight I managed to force my adversary nearly to the ground, but without putting him out of action. The strong and gusty wind had driven the enemy plane over our lines. My adversary tried by flying over trees and other obstacles to escape. Then I forced him to land in the village of Farbus where the machine smashed against a house. The observer kept on shooting until the machine touched ground.* **99**

The B.E.2d flown by Lt. J. C. Powell and Air/Mech. P. Bonner, both of whom were killed, bore the serial number 5841. By this time, Manfred's brother Lothar had joined Jasta 11, using influence that came from fame and not rank. Manfred had a great affection for his younger brother and felt more secure with him around. He could keep an eye on him, ensure he got the best encouragement and learn to fight the way Manfred wanted him to. Above all, Manfred felt he at last had a confidant that was closer to him than any of the friends who came and went. They certainly had their differences but the brothers shared their thoughts and their fears.

Thrust into the melee of the rank and file in a closely knit unit where camaraderie was an important part of efficiency, Manfred was ill at ease and longed for the more autocratic way of life he had been brought up to expect. These factors and other tensions brought about through continuous exposure to danger and combat sometimes blurred reality, and imagination played a big part in memory when it came to piecing together the facts of an actual engagement. A classic example of that in von Richthofen's short but furious life occurred on the afternoon of April 2.

After attacking a Sopwith 1 1/2 Strutter flown by 2nd/Lt. P. Warren and Sgt. R. Dunn from No. 43 Sqdn, RFC, von Richthofen claimed in his combat report that he forced the aircraft **66** *to land 300 metres east of Givenchy. But as my adversary would not surrender and even as his machine was on the ground, he kept shooting at me, thereby hitting my machine very severely at an altitude of 5 metres. I once more attacked him and killed one of the occupants.* **99** This is at variance with the account rendered by von Richthofen in his book *Der Rote Kampfflieger* written several months later. There he recalls that Werner Voss was witness to his restraint as he refrained from firing back at the downed aircraft even when fired upon by the observer on the ground.

Did von Richthofen deliberately fire upon an injured man on the ground? If so, he was surely within his rights to defend himself and prevent his Albatros from receiving a hit or worse.

66 *Suddenly, we saw an English air patrol approaching from the other side...Although there were nine Englishmen, and although they were on their own territory, they preferred to avoid battle...Nevertheless, we caught up with them...I was nearest to the enemy and attacked the man at the rear of the formation. To my great delight, I noticed that he accepted battle, and my pleasure increased when I discovered that his comrades deserted him, so I had once more a single fight.*

A favourable wind came to my aid, and it drove both of us over the German lines...At last I hit him. I noticed a ribbon of white vapour. He would have to land for his motor had stopped...When he had come to the ground, I flew over him...He levelled his machine gun and shot holes into my machine. Afterward Voss told me that if that had happened to him, he would have shot him on the ground. As a matter of fact I ought to have done so, for he had not surrendered. **99**

1917

"On this day, our group had been assigned to an early morning start, that is to say, it had to be prepared to take to the air first at any moment. Our duty began between 4:00 am and 5:00 am. We had just got up and were sitting in the starting house, when the telephone rang. "Six Bristols coming across from Arras in the direction of Douai" was the message.

We jumped into our planes and started. High up above us at about 9,000 ft there was a broken cover of clouds. We could see the English planes below the clouds not far from our aerodrome. My brother's red bird was standing ready at the doors of its hangar, but my brother was not to be seen."
Lothar von Richthofen

April 2 1917

"We came into contact with the enemy, but the Englishmen were too clever with their machines, and we could not bring any of them down. Whenever we thought we had one of them, he disappeared in the clouds. After flying around for an hour without having brought down a single plane, we flew back and landed.

My brother's red plane was in the open hangar door, apparently in the same spot where we had last seen it, but anyone could see, judging from the activity of the mechanics working on it, that it had been up in the air. We asked the mechanics.

They told us the Lieutenant had left the ground five minutes after we had started, and that he had returned twenty minutes later, after having brought down an English plane. We walked back to our quarters and found that my brother had gone back to bed and was sleeping as though nothing had happened."
Lothar von Richthofen

April 2 1917

If he did not, why did he say he did? And did the observer, Sgt. Dunn, actually fire back at the low flying scout plane? While still alive just after the war, the surviving pilot, 2nd/Lt. P. Warren, firmly denied that Dunn was in any fit condition to fire his gun. Dying from a severe wound in his abdomen, Dunn almost certainly could not have mustered the strength to fire and Warren says that he certainly had no time to use the gun. Moreover, he cannot remember any shots from anywhere after they crash landed.

But why should von Richthofen make two opposing statements presenting each as the truth? The possibility exists that he was in a state of obsessive hypertension at the end of the duel and that he firmly believed that he was being fired at. It is not uncommon for a related sound, heard soon after a period of great danger and concentration, to trigger a belief that threats immediately preceding the experience are still present. Pilots were constantly under the greatest pressure it is possible to regularly subject men to while expecting them to retain a measure of sanity.

In all probability von Richthofen genuinely believed he was being fired upon and he may even have involuntarily fired back; Warren was in no state to identify machine gun fire from a low flying aircraft amid the noise and the fury of combat. Did Manfred's close friend Werner Voss, watching from above, persuade him of the way it actually happened so that his book carries at least a partial truth? We shall never know.

Next day, April 3, von Richthofen shot down a F.E.2d from No. 25 Sqdn, RFC, flown by 2nd/Lt. D. P. McDonald and 2nd/Lt. J. I. M. O'Beirne, in the company of his brother Lothar and Lt. Karl Schaeffer who had joined Jasta 11 shortly after Manfred arrived to command the unit. The pressure to defeat the enemy was hotting up and from March 22, von Richthofen had been promoted to Oberleutnant. The new year was bringing much greater opportunity for combat. The single-seat scout was now a firmly established aircraft type and increasing numbers of German and British machines filled the skies. This year, 1917, would see the definitive World War I fighters emerge to support a dramatic increase in air power and aerial combat.

CHAPTER SEVEN *A Flying Circus*

Von Richthofen's 35th victory was one of the new Bristol F.2A biplanes in which the British had placed great faith. It was attained during the morning of April 5. There was fog on the ground and mist at altitude as four Albatros scouts of Jasta 11 swooped unobserved upon six two-seat F.2As from No. 48 Sqdn, RFC. Led by Capt W. Leefe-Robinson who, as a Lieutenant, on the night of September 2/3, 1916, shot down the first Zeppelin over English soil, the F.2A biplanes were flown like two-seater reconnaissance aircraft defending themselves from attack.

Instead of using the forward firing machine gun as a defensive weapon and pointing the aircraft at the enemy, leaving the rear gunner to defend the tail area, the pilots manoeuvred their machines to give the observer the primary field of fire. This resulted in a chaotic situation where the aircraft was vulnerable to attack from the front, the side and the rear and unable to properly defend itself from either gun position. Of the six Bristols, one was immediately driven down by von Richthofen, two more were shot down by the other members of Jasta 11 and fifteen minutes after the first enagegment von Richthofen got a second F.2A which was forced to land near Quincy.

On the basis of this limited experience, von Richthofen claimed the Albatros as **undoubtedly superior in both speed and ability to climb**. The Bristol Fighter, as it became known, was not the failure this first experience indicated it to be and improvements over the next few weeks provided an aircraft that was to remain in service with the British for fifteen years. The pasting given by von Richthofen and his Jasta 11 was reciprocated, with little result, during that night. Eleven British

The second of April, 1917, was a very warm day for my Jagdstaffel. From my quarters I could clearly hear the drum of fire, which was again particularly violent. I was still in bed when my orderly rushed into the room and exclaimed: "Sir, the English are here!"

Sleepy as I was, I looked out of the window, and there were my dear friends circling over the flying ground. I jumped out of bed and into my clothes in a jiffy. My red bird had been pulled out of the hangars and was ready for starting. My mechanics knew that I would probably not allow such a favourable moment to go by unused. Everything was ready. I snatched up my furs and went up.

Suddenly, one of the impertinent Englishmen tried to drop down upon me...I realised quite soon that I was his master and that he could not escape me...The Englishman defended himself up to the last moment... I was delighted with the performance of my red machine, and returned to the aerodrome. My comrades were still in the air, and they were surprised when we met later at breakfast and I told that I had scored my thirty-second machine.

April 1917

"I was already in bed fast asleep when I heard, as though in a dream, anti-aircraft firing. I awoke to find the dream a reality. One of the Englishmen at that moment was flying so low over my quarters that, in my sudden fright, I pulled the blankets over my head. The next moment, I heard an incredible bang just outside my window. The glass fell in, a victim to the bomb. I rushed out of my bedroom in pyjamas in order to get a few shots in after him, but unfortunately I had overslept my opportunity. He was being fired on from everywhere."

1917

Below
April 1917 and a selection of Jasta 11 pilots gather for the camera: (left to right) Hartmann, Plueschow, Krefft, Simon, Wolff, Esser, Manfred von Richthofen, Lothar von Richthofen, Hintsch, Brauneck, Matthof and Allmenroeder.

F.E.2bs tried to bomb Douai airfield, rousing Manfred from sleep but causing amusement as the lumbering biplanes searched for targets on the ground below. They did remarkably well, however, found the airfield in the dark and dropped a large number of small Cooper bombs but without seriously disrupting the operational capability of Jasta 11.

Von Richthofen mused on their vulnerability and had machine guns set up on posts as a basic form of anti-aircraft defence. Next night, the preparations complete, Jasta 11 was ready for the bombers but they did not come until the night of the 7th April, the day von Richthofen had scored another victory edging closer all the time to the 40 victories achieved by Oswald Boelcke, the leading German ace. The victory that day has been contested by some who find insufficient evidence that von Richthofen actually shot down the Nieuport 17 of No. 60 Sqdn, RFC, he claimed:

"With four of my gentlemen I attacked an enemy squadron of six Nieuport machines south of Arras and behind the enemy lines. The plane I singled out tried to escape six times and by various manoeuvres. When he was doing this for the seventh time, I managed to hit him, whereupon the engine began to smoke and the plane went down head first, twisting and turning. At first I thought it was another manoeuvre, but then I saw that the plane dashed to the ground without catching itself near Mercatel."

It was 5:45 pm and the pilot was 2nd/Lt. G. O. Smart. He was killed in the resulting crash. That night the F.E.2bs came again to Douai but despite the defences only one aircraft was lost and although other visits were made later in the month no significant results were achieved. The British had hoped to put Jasta 11 out of action temporarily if not permanently. Under von Richthofen's tutelage they were becoming an elite fighting unit and although the edicts were very different to the dicta of Boelcke the pilots were certainly achieving a masterful command of the air war on the Arras sector. Achievements came thick and fast and none more fruitfully than those now logged up by von Richthofen.

On April 8, he shot down two aircraft. At 11:40 am **With three of my planes I attacked three Sopwiths above Farbus. The plane I singled out went into a right hand spiral downwards. The observer ceased firing. I followed my adversary to the ground where he was dashed to pieces.** That was a Sopwith 1 1/2 Strutter flown by Lt. J. S. Heagerty and Lt. L. H. Cantle. Just five hours later, **I was flying and surprised an English artillery flyer. After a few shots the plane broke into pieces and fell near Vimy, on this side of the lines.** Thus ended the lives of 2nd/Lt. K. I. Mackensie and 2nd/Lt. G. Everingham flying their B.E.2e of No. 16 Sqdn, RFC.

The day von Richthofen got his 38th and 39th victories, there was another near fatal accident at Jasta 11 when the port lower wing of Vizefeldwebel Festner's Albatros D.III collapsed at 13,000 ft. With skilful airmanship, the pilot managed to nurse it down to a safe landing and present for inspection an intact Albatros D.III that had survived wing failure. There were too many incidents like this and von Richthofen knew that safe, reliable machines were essential if his men were to have confidence in their aircraft. He wrote a stiff memo outlining essential characteristics for a new fighter, assets deemed lacking in the Albatros.

The manufacturer had, meanwhile, been working on the basic D.III design and was about to introduce the D.V. With an oval cross-section fuselage replacing the slab-sided fuselage of the D.III, the new aircraft would be little better than its predecessor. The reason for continued wing failure would not be properly understood for some time and this frustrated the better pilots and angered Manfred von Richthofen. The pilots knew only too well that the Albatros scouts could not be dived to terminal speed with any guarantee they would survive the strain. Moreover, new British and French aircraft were coming into use that performed better than the Albatros.

To the Engineer Department, Berlin, Adlershof. Via C.O. Air Forces, 6th Army. Subject: Breaking of wing of Albatros D.III 2-23-16

On April 8th, 1917, Sergeant Festner's machine broke its left lower wing at an altitude of 13,000 ft without previous straining. In spite of the fact that the wing was torn to pieces and diminished by more than one third of its surface, Sergeant Festner is submitting a detailed report of how it happened. Technical examination: From the second rib up to the V strut, the lower surface was folded upward. Cause: breaking of ribs. Locality of the break: entirely near the forward part of the wing, where the factory had applied special rib-supporting braces. The fabric covering of the wings was torn to pieces by the current of air through the broken parts. The naked wing was thus strained in front by the wind, causing it to bend backward and then to move loosely frontward again. This, of course, was too much strain for the V strut. The machine is being sent home as useless for warfare.
Freiherr von Richthofen

April 1917

Responding to the appearance in 1916 of new and superior German fighting scouts, the British Sopwith company came up with the Triplane, a fighting aircraft with a remarkable rate of roll and fast climb due largely to its three wings. The Sopwith Triplanes of the RNAS were to play a part in the von Richthofen myth for all time. It was the appearance of the astoundingly successful British 'Dreidecker' on the Western Front that inspired a spate of triplanes from German manufacturers eager to emulate what they considered a magic formula for superior performance: three parallel wings set on a short fuselage. Thus, by autumn 1917, the Fokker triplane was set to appear in front line units.

Three days after his April 8 double, von Richthofen shot down his 40th official victim to equal Boelcke's score. It was a B.E.2c flown by Lt. E. C. E. Derwin and Gnr. H. Pierson of No. 13 Sqdn, RFC, which fell into a shell hole from which the aviators were saved by advancing British troops. Two days later, Manfred got his first triple victory taking him well clear of the previous record for the highest scoring German air ace. The first came at the precisely reported time of 8:58 am when an R.E.8 carrying Capt. J. Stuart and Lt. M. H. Wood of No. 59 Sqdn, RFC, was destroyed. The second came at 12:45 pm and was a F.E.2b from No. 25 Sqdn, RFC, possibly carrying Sgt. J. Cunliffe and 2nd A/M W. J. Bolton, while the third, also a F.E.2b from the same squadron, fell near Henin-Lietard killing 2nd/Lt. A. H. Bates and Sgt. W. A. Barnes.

Von Richthofen had not encountered an R.E.8 before although the first of this type had appeared in November 1916, and would come to be seen in increasing numbers during 1917. Similar in appearance to the B.E.2, the R.E.8 was no match at all for the nifty German scouts. Five Jasta 11 pilots shot down all six R.E.8s they encountered that morning. Only when engaged by aircraft of their own type were the fighter pilots of the Jagdstaffeln on fair and equal terms. Next day there was a positively unequal balance between antagonists when von Richthofen and his Jasta attacked five Nieuports which were preying on a German two-seat reconnaissance machine. A lucky hit from the two-seater damaged the engine of Nieuport A6796 so that when von Richthofen attacked it was already going down. Forced to the ground, its pilot taken prisoner, Manfred was credited with this as his 44th official victory.

The carnage continued. On April 16, a B.E.2c found spotting for the artillery at just under 3,000 feet was attacked killing the observer, Lt. C. E. Wilson, and so badly wounding the pilot Lt. W. Green that a broken leg was left unset in the belief that he

" Among the chief properties of a good fighter plane are the following: A good plane must lose altitude when curving and after flying and turning several times on its back, provided of course, the motor is doing full speed. It would be ideal if a plane could even gain in altitude while performing these manoeuvres, but this is not the case with the Albatros D.III, and that is its chief drawback.

When moving the side or altitude rudders, even the slightest change must effect a big movement. With the Albatros, the ailerons are not quite sufficient, and this is a most important factor with a fighter plane. Great speed and great altitude are both necessary. To be able to fly slowly by regulating the motor is very essential. A fighter plane must be able to stand the strain of diving down 3,000 ft. The Albatros does not always do this."

was going to die. He did not die and after six weeks the doctors broke his uselessly crooked leg but pinned it incorrectly. It had to be broken again and re-pinned at a different angle but it never again gave Willie Green the normal use of his legs. He could not even remember the reason. Crushed at the base, his skull was so badly damaged that all memory of the fight had been wiped clean.

The weather was bad on the Western Front and not before the 22nd did von Richthofen get his next victory. *66 When my Staffel was engaging an enemy squadron, I personally attacked the last of the aircraft. Immediately after I had discharged my first shots the plane began to smoke. After 500 shots it dashed down and crashed to splinters on the ground.99* Lt. W. F. Fletcher and Lt. W. Franklin escaped with their lives and as the aircraft had drifted westward from Lagnicourt they were on British occupied soil. The following day, von Richthofen's next victims were not so lucky. Flying a B.E.2e, 2nd/Lt. E. A. Welch and Sgt. A. Tollervey were killed when the wings on their biplane came off and the wreckage fell near Mericourt.

On April 23 also, Manfred wrote to his mother saying how much he looked forward to his vacation, and to honouring an invitation to meet the Kaiser. He noted that Lothar had scored 10 victories and that Jasta 11 had notched up 100 confirmed kills since he came to lead them just over three months before. Motivated by the welcome rest and an opportunity to hunt and enjoy life for a while, Manfred threw himself into a frenzy of activity. On April 28 he shot down a B.E.2e flown by Lt. R. W. Follit and 2nd/Lt. F. J. Kirkham which, he proudly noted in the combat report, *66 was never able to get out of range of my guns.99*

On April 29, just two days before going on leave, he scored four victories, beginning at 12:05 pm with a Spad S.7 piloted by the inexperienced Lt. R. Applin, continuing with a F.E.2b at 4:55 pm flown by Sgt. G. Stead and Cpl. A. Beebee, a B.E.2d at 7:25 pm and a Nieuport 17 at 7:40 pm from No. 40 Sqdn, RFC, piloted by Capt. F. L. Barwell. To cap the day, Lothar was credited with two kills, bringing his total to 19 and the von Richthofen brothers' grand score to 71! All this, under the admiring gaze of Major Albrecht Freiherr von Richthofen who was visiting Jasta 11 to see his sons in action. Manfred had 52 confirmed victories and could go on vacation confident that he had amply exceeded Boelcke's score.

But Manfred had the nagging suspicion that his younger brother would outdo him and that thought alone had spurred him on

66 Dear Mother:

I intend to come home at the beginning of May, but before then I will go pheasant shooting, to which I have been invited and to which I am looking forward eagerly. After that I have been invited to lunch with the Kaiser. Meanwhile, my forty-fourth stands to my credit, but I will take a rest after the first half-century. Lothar has had his tenth victory. Since I took over this command, it has accounted for one hundred planes. Uncle Lex will visit me during the next few days. Wedel was here too, and apart from them the house is continuously crowded with guests.99

April 23 1917

Decorations

Throughout his illustrious career as a fighter pilot and as a unit and group field commander, von Richthofen was awarded medals from several countries actively supporting the German cause. Many were gratuitious and a mark of general recognition rather than a specific event. Such was the Pour le Merite which, unlike the British Victoria Cross or the French Medaille Militaire, was awarded for having reached a level of achievement deserving the highest recognition. It was also given to von Richthofen because the public expected the High Command to recognise him, and acknowledge his achievements, in this way. This had the added advantage in giving the government propaganda department added reason to give von Richthofen greater attention and so bolster public support at home. Other medals were awarded by friendly countries who recognised in von Richthofen an asset vital for public support of the increasingly hungry war machine.

GERMAN DECORATIONS:

Iron Cross Second Class
Iron Cross First Class
Pour le Merite
Order of the House of Hohenzollern
Order of the Royal House of Oldenburg
Saxony Military Order of St. Henry
Griffon Cross
Hessen Order of Phillips
Saxe-Coburg-Gotha Duke Karl Edward Medal
Lippe Schaumberg Cross
Bremen Hanseatic Cross
Lubeck Hanseatic Cross

AUSTRO-HUNGARIAN DECORATIONS:

Order of the Holy Crown
Imperial Order of the Iron Crown
Military Service Cross

« Dear Mamma:

I suppose you will be angry with me for having been in Germany for eight days without dropping you a line. I am shooting pheasants here, and expect to remain here until the fourteenth. The sport is wonderful. After that, I have to go to Berlin to look over the new planes. That will take me about three days, and then for Schweidnitz. Until then you will have to excuse me. From Schweidnitz I will ride over to the Prince of Pless's estate and bag an elk there. Toward the end of the month, I will look over the other fronts, the Balkans, etc. That will take from three to four weeks. In the meantime, Lothar is commanding my squadron and is I think, down for the Pour le Merite. How do you like your two bad boys? »

May 9 1917

BULGARIAN DECORATIONS:

Order of Military Valour

TURKISH DECORATIONS:

Star of Gallipoli
Imtjaz Medal
Liakat Medal

Awarded by order of the Kaiser from January 1913, the "Badge for Military Pilots" (below left) was given to officers, NCOs and aviators who received their pilot's wings. It came with a certificate and depicted a biplane flying across country with rural scenes below. Topped with a crown, the badge was made

from silver and carried a retaining clasp for attachment to the wearer's tunic. It was about 70 mm high and 43 mm wide. Some were given to foreign pilots of friendly nations. Most German air aces began their flying career serving as observers. Carried across the battle lines by pilots thought of as "chauffeurs", they bore the brunt of the daily war chores. German officers assigned to these duties, and who completed more than 1,000 km of reconnaissance flying were given the Observer badge (left). It was introduced in January 1914, by order of the Kaiser and was about the same size as the pilot's badge. For meritorious action some aviators were given the Honour Goblet (above) and certificate. This particular award was given to Lt Hans Pippart who had scored 22 victories at the time of his death on August 11, 1918, elevating him to 59th in the list of German air aces.

The Blue Max

To a German aviator of World War I, the most coveted award was the Ordre Pour le Merite. Known as the Blue Max, it was given for acts of bravery and meritorious achievement. The Ordre was established in 1740 by Frederick the Great and inscribed with an F. It was in French because that was the language of the Prussian court. Manfred von Richthofen (above) proudly wears his medal in this familiar propaganda picture, thousands of which were circulated when he became one of Germany's notable air aces. In all, 81 air aces received the medal while a further 19 were awarded the Ordre Pour le Merite but failed to receive it.

With little appearance of the bold fighter ace he would become, Manfred von Richthofen at the age of two years wears the hair style and dress of late 19th century Silesia.

Family Matters

The young von Richthofen was brought up to honour his family and express a sense of pride and honesty, important qualities which were to stand him in good stead. His interpretation of absolute truth absolves him of the dishonesty not uncommon in victory claimants; when the young fighter pilot claimed to have shot down an enemy aeroplane he believed he really had. Yet for all the dash and verve of his military career, he was a family man too. Manfred relaxes (top right) with his mother, his sister Ilse and brother Bolko. Above, the cat mascot that would survive him and the bungalow building that served as home at an airfield on the Western Front, a far cry from the home he had been brought up in as a young boy before the rigours of cadet school. His mother (right) survived her husband and her two sons Manfred and Lothar before she died in western Europe, far from the home where Germany's greatest World War I air ace had grown up. At far right, one of the many portraits for the public.

Rittmeister Manfred Frhr. von Richthofen

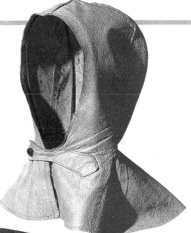

The helmet worn by Manfred von Richthofen bears the marks of use. Open and exposed in the air to wind and rain, cockpits were not the sophisticated enclosures occupied by today's airmen. Clothing was all important.

A father comes to see his son in the Hospital of St Nicholas in Courtrai after Manfred fell from the sky in combat on July 6, 1917, and received a head wound.

Trophies adorn Manfred's room at home with numbers removed from some of the aeroplanes he shot down. Note the rotary engine adapted as a light and the memorabilia adorning the room. Grisly reminders of death and carnage that stalked the warriors of aerial combat. It would not be long before Manfred's own possessions were sought by collectors.

Manfred and Lothar (above) in relaxed pose. Fellow pilots (left to right) Festner, Schaeffer, Manfred, Lothar and Wolff of Jasta 11, the last three of which would claim a total 153 victories.

Triplane Myth

The popular belief that von Richthofen was most frequently seen flying a Fokker Dr.I Triplane is completely incorrect. In fact, only 19 of his 80 confirmed victories were achieved with aircraft of this type. The majority of von Richthofen's victims fell to the guns of his Albatros scout aircraft, a type he first used for his first official victory on September 17, 1916. Seen here (right), with Manfred in the cockpit and Lothar seated cross-legged in front, the Albatros was in some respects superior to the Triplane, which did not enter service before late August 1917, and by April 1918 had been largely replaced by the Fokker D.VII. Another myth involving the Triplane derived from rumours about its origin, for it was the British that first spurred development of the Fokker design. The Sopwith Triplane (opposite page) was introduced by the British in early 1917 and after von Richthofen reported favourably on its performance when engaged in battle, German manufacturers generated a plethora of Triplanes, Anthony Fokker's being the most successful.

The Legacy

No surviving Fokker triplane exists today in flying condition. Moreover, the ravages of time and the devastation caused by second World War have left no surviving example that could be brought to flying condition. Yet the magic that surrounds the type and the mystery that still haunts the legend of Manfred von Richthofen has tempted several specialists to build replicas.

The replica seen here is one of several that over the years have graced the skies of Europe and North America. The engine is very different from the Le Rhone or Oberursel that powered the original more than 70 years ago but pilots testify to the remarkable agility and manoeuvrability possessed by the DR.1. Characteristics inherent in the design which first took to the air in 1917.

Seen here with Anthony Fokker at the wheel, Manfred von Richthofen joins the Dutchman in his car during one of their many meetings to discuss plans for the new Fokker Triplane which the German ace was to do so much to immortalise. Without von Richthofen's patronage, the odd little aircraft would not have received the fame it did and few today would remember it.

Air combat in the 1914-18 war progressed with the development of fighting scouts, later known simply as "fighters". From the Vickers F.B.5 Gunbus (right) to the faster and more effective Sopwith Pup (top right) the fighting aeroplane was transformed from an aircraft with a gun for defence to a fighting machine with forward firing guns and higher performance. Men like von Richthofen exploited the advances in design of airframes and engines, encouraging the manufacturers to try new concepts, like the Triplane (above), epitomised here by the aircraft flown by Lt Werner Voss.

Open cockpits and total exposure to the elements required pilots and air crew to wear protective clothing. Experience and a demand for better protection resulted in total enclosure in leather gear.

Adequate protection against the bitter cold of flying on the Western Front was frequently a matter of finding the right kind of clothing. Here, Manfred gets dressed for combat during late summer 1917, a dressing on his head wound visible beneath his cap. Pilots frequently used ladders to reach the cockpit despite Hollywood images showing flyers leaping into their planes!

With 0.303 in calibre, the Lewis gun was selected by many British aeroplane builders for scout as well as reconnaissance types.

A Royal Flying Corps cap typical of the informal head dress worn in the British air arm before it became the Royal Air Force in April 1918.

No effort was made to cover the cockpits of operational World War I fighters, despite several experimental designs. This S.E.5 cockpit typifies the elementary nature of controls and displays available to the fighting airman.

A full head and neck helmet (left) worn by air crew serving in the Royal Flying Corps during World War I with fur lining and an opening for the eyes. The Austro-Hungarian Luftfahrtruppen, a major ally, had its own badges and insignia. The Austrian pilots badge (above left) comprised a green enamel wreath. German air gunners badges (above right) are now rare items.

One of the most informal and pleasing photographs of von Richthofen taken at a forward airfield.

Overleaf
One of the most important air duels in Manfred von Richthofen's career took place on November 23, 1916, resulting in his 11th officially credited victory. Seen here in a unique interpretation by aviation artist Michael Roffe, are the last few minutes in the life of Maj. Lanoe George Hawker of the Royal Flying Corps as he was pursued by von Richthofen in his Albatros D.II. Contrary to the myth, von Richthofen was not flying an all-red Albatros, in fact the aircraft probably did not depart from the standard colour as depicted here. The duel began at 8,000 ft when von Richthofen engaged two D.H.2s, one flown by Hawker. Von Richthofen fought long and hard to gain the upper hand but found the experienced Hawker a fair match. The fight ended at low altitude when the German ace shot Hawker through the head about 100 ft above the ground. Hawker was a well respected pilot, holder of the Victoria Cross.

MICHAEL ROFFE

Few aeroplanes have evoked more emotion than the all-red Triplane flown by Manfred von Richthofen from early September 1917, with very little interval until his death in April 1918. In fact, his last 17 victories were scored on Triplanes. In all, von Richthofen flew Triplanes with serial numbers 102/17, 127/17, 152/17, 425/17 and 477/17. It was in 477/17 that he scored 9 victories but it was while flying 425/17 (depicted here) that he met his end. Between the end of October and mid-December 1917, the Triplane was grounded following two fatal accidents caused by poor workmanship. Nevertheless, the aircraft was a success with the leading air aces largely because their experience permitted optimum use of the aircraft's better qualities: handling, agility and good rate of climb. But it was not fast and several two-seat reconnaissance planes could outrun the Fokker Triplane. Not a lot were built, only 320 being ordered, all in 1917. In all, the Dr.I had little impact on the air war and in view of the much greater numbers of Albatros and Pfalz fighters, it hardly credits a mention — were it not (of course) for its patronage by Manfred von Richthofen and a few equals.

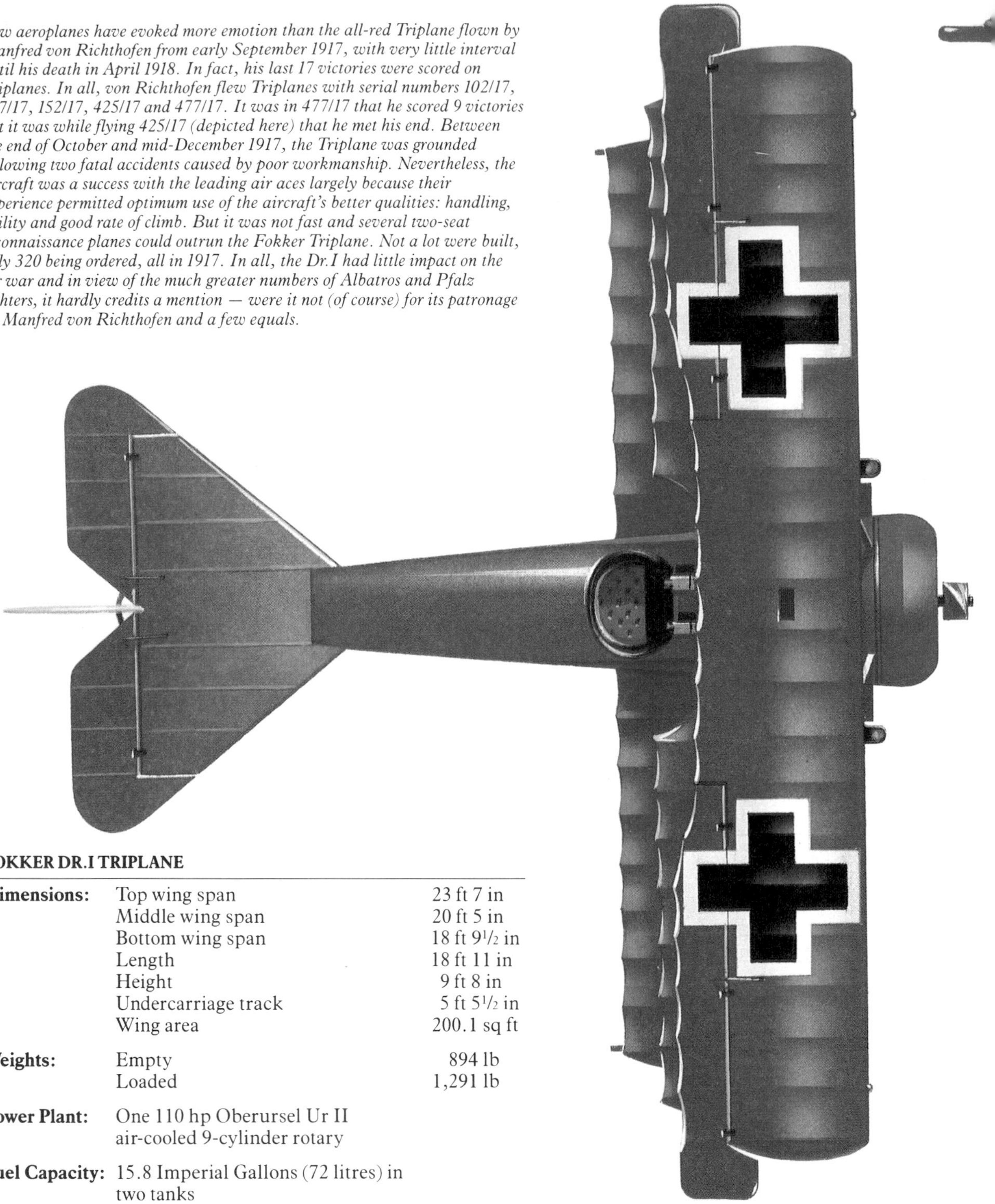

FOKKER DR.I TRIPLANE

Dimensions:	Top wing span	23 ft 7 in
	Middle wing span	20 ft 5 in
	Bottom wing span	18 ft 9½ in
	Length	18 ft 11 in
	Height	9 ft 8 in
	Undercarriage track	5 ft 5½ in
	Wing area	200.1 sq ft
Weights:	Empty	894 lb
	Loaded	1,291 lb
Power Plant:	One 110 hp Oberursel Ur II air-cooled 9-cylinder rotary	
Fuel Capacity:	15.8 Imperial Gallons (72 litres) in two tanks	
Armament:	Two fixed 7.92 mm Spandau LMG 08/15 machine guns	

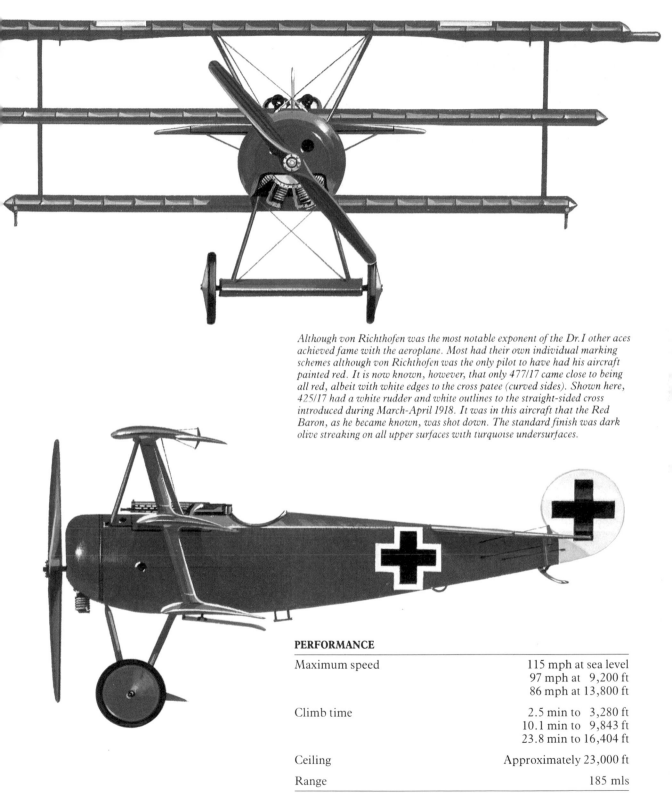

Although von Richthofen was the most notable exponent of the Dr.I other aces achieved fame with the aeroplane. Most had their own individual marking schemes although von Richthofen was the only pilot to have had his aircraft painted red. It is now known, however, that only 477/17 came close to being all red, albeit with white edges to the cross patee (curved sides). Shown here, 425/17 had a white rudder and white outlines to the straight-sided cross introduced during March-April 1918. It was in this aircraft that the Red Baron, as he became known, was shot down. The standard finish was dark olive streaking on all upper surfaces with turquoise undersurfaces.

PERFORMANCE

Maximum speed	115 mph at sea level
	97 mph at 9,200 ft
	86 mph at 13,800 ft
Climb time	2.5 min to 3,280 ft
	10.1 min to 9,843 ft
	23.8 min to 16,404 ft
Ceiling	Approximately 23,000 ft
Range	185 mls

Craftsmanship

When aeroplanes were first used as weapons
of war it was because they were believed to be
of value for advancing armies and for
scouting the whereabouts of enemy forces.
Gradually, between 1914 and 1916, they were
developed into indigenous fighting machines
which would serve as mounts for air aces and
as bomb carriers to hit supply lines and troop
concentrations far behind the lines. Because
the role of the aeroplane became increasingly
important, the attention to detail in design
and manufacture was paramount. Using
cabinet makers and women skilled in working
with linen and fabric, the wooden aeroplanes
were crafted with care and diligence.
Workshops were a vital part of front-line
aviation because aircraft were frequently
damaged and repairs in the field were a vital
part of maintaining operational readiness.

Vulnerability was a major problem for the flyers of World War I and no less a hazard for the airframes and engines. Exposed, with little or no protection to the elements, gun fire from the ground or attacking fighters intent on destroying enemy planes, aircraft and aircrew stood little or no chance of survival. Control systems (right) were little changed since the pre-war days and manufacturing was biased toward maximum rates of production. The finish looked good but some corners were cut when manufacturers substituted poor quality products in attempts to maximise profits. But cases of bad workmanship were few and far between. Most notable were defects in Fokker aircraft which more than once came under the eye of the Inspectorate when wings came off and spars failed without warning, the Triplane being a case in point.

Enemy fighters were a constant threat to bombers and reconnaissance aircraft. Built by the British, the Sopwith Camel (above) epitomised the fighter pilot's dream. Fast, manoeuvrable and equipped with two machine guns synchronised to fire forward through the propeller arc, it was not suitable for the novice. Many inexperienced pilots got to fly the Camel because they had little or no time to become familiar with less sprightly machines before transitioning to the Camel. It was a Sopwith Camel of No. 209 Sqdn. RAF that attacked von Richthofen on the morning of April 21, 1918, when he was engaging another Camel during the chase that led to his death. The Camel was strong and agile but prone to spring surprises on the inexperienced pilot. Temperamental and notorious among those who came to fly it, the Camel was immortalised by several famous World War I pilots. It could out turn any German fighter in the sky but if handled without respect would throw pilot and machine into a dangerous spin. More than 5,400 Sopwith Camels were built and along with the S.E.5 it became the most famous aeroplane of World War I, shooting down a total 1,294 enemy aircraft.

The stress of flying war planes in World War 1 brought a morbid sense of fate and most flyers expected to be shot down at least once during their tour of duty. A few were convinced they would be killed and Manfred von Richthofen was no exception. In fact he made ample preparation for the day he would die and wrote instructions in a letter about who should succeed him.

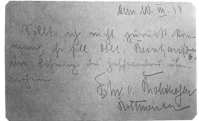

Instructions like these were common, especially from officers like von Richthofen with responsibilities for four Jasta.

Controversy for a long time surrounded the engine fitted to von Richthofen's Dr.I on the day he crashed and was killed. It was at first believed to have been a 110 hp Le Rhone type built under licence in Sweden but a manufacturers plate attached to the engine when the Triplane was recovered showed it to have been made in Frankfurt, confirming it to be a 100 hp Oberursel. Some engines were

built by the Thulin firm in Sweden but this was not one of them. Pilots preferred the Swedish built motors and did all in their power to get one. The plate attached to von Richthofen's engine was stolen soon after it was first displayed so the exact details are not known. The engine is held today by the Imperial War Museum, London, where the photographs on this page were taken. It was thoroughly cleaned for the first time in 1989, revealing the mud of war from the Somme valley still clinging to its exterior surfaces.

Souvenir hunters had a field day with von Richthofen's Triplane although many more claims exist than can possibly be substantiated. For instance, there is sufficient fabric to cover a dozen Triplanes!

Scavenged

Von Richthofen met his death in Fokker Dr.I 425/17 with the factory number (2009/18) marked clearly on the interplane struts. For a while, the factory number was quoted, as the serial number applied when the Dr.I was ordered and delivered for service use. Scavenged for souvenirs, little remained of the Triplane, not even a piece of fabric bearing its serial number. In the haste to adorn their shelves and cabinets, English and Australian aviators stripped von Richthofen's aircraft. In much the same way the German pilot had sought to collect the spoils of war from his defeated victims, so too did the avengers pillage the aeroplane in which von Richthofen met his death. The remains were held by No. 3 Sqdn. Australian Flying Corps, its personnel seen here inspecting the rear fuselage and tail along with the two Spandau machine guns fired by von Richthofen for the last time on April 21, 1918. The Australians preserved the compass, a piece of the propeller and the control column. They also obtained the fur lined flying boots used by von Richthofen.

Last Post

Manfred von Richthofen was shot down at approximately 10.45 am, April 21, 1918. His body was recovered from no-man's land by Air Mechanic C. C. Collins before dark fell, and during late afternoon the following day he was buried with full military honours at a small cemetery in the French village of Bertangles. A 12-man party from No. 3 Sqdn. Australian Flying Corps fired a salute.

Tribute

A vanquished foe in war, von Richthofen was a respected fellow airman in death and his loss was recognised by both sides. On a cross made from a cut-down four-bladed propeller were inscribed the words:

CAVALRY CAPTAIN
MANFRED BARON VON RICHTHOFEN
*Age 22 years, killed in aerial combat near
Sailly-Le-Sac*
SOMME, FRANCE, 21st APRIL, 1918

He was, in fact, almost 26 when he died. The inset picture shows what remains today of the Red Baron's grave in Bertangles.

furiously as, in the weeks before his vacation, he watched Lothar's score mount up. In the first month of active duty at the front, Lothar von Richthofen shot down 20 aircraft. His fear in 1915 that Lothar would excel himself before he could achieve distinction led Manfred to seek liberation from trench war and seek satisfaction in the air. Now, the fear that in his chosen domain the rising spectre of his brother's performance may yet threaten his own lofty achievement was a constant concern to him. For a while, however, he would be about other business while Lothar ran Jasta 11.

Manfred left Douai in a two-seat D.F.W.CV piloted by Lt. Krefft, who was also going on leave. Only the previous evening a telephone call to his airfield told Manfred to meet the Kaiser two days hence after a special briefing at General Headquarters on May 1. There was no time to lose. There was much to prepare for. In the last two months, Manfred's score, and consequently his claim to fame, had more than doubled. First, a public reception at Cologne where he was feted with flowers and town dignatories. Then, a meeting with General von Hoeppner, the General Officer Commanding the German Air Service.

Manfred saw the Kaiser on his 25th birthday, having been introduced to Field Marshal von Hindenburg and General Erich Ludendorff. He graciously accepted a bust of the Emperor and dined that evening at a lavish feast hosted by von Hindenburg. The following day Manfred was again flown by Krefft in the CV, this time to meet the Empress at Bad Homburg and be enthusiastically received by lesser mortals among the local estate workers. Official duties over, Krefft was allowed to leave for his own vacation while Manfred went to the Black Forest in search of game. After that, a visit to some other flying units and new aircraft being tested at Adlershof, Berlin, until finally he was given a warm welcome at home in Schweidnitz.

From his visit to General Headquarters he learned of great things planned for 1918. Of a massive push that would overwhelm the enemy's combined forces before American troops could make a significant impact. Von Richthofen knew there would be hard days ahead and that much would depend on the speed with which the war could be brought to an honourable end. But he was not deluded into thinking Germany would prevail and confided to his mother that they would not win the war. Whether the tedium of working on his autobiography finally drove him to the Pless Estates, or the possibility of bagging more game drew him to the lush countryside, Manfred arrived on May 26 to sample delights usually preserved for the Kaiser. He shot bison and bagged them with considerable skill.

In an opportune moment during a visit to Headquarters, the Prince of Pless invited me to hunt bison with him. The bison is the animal which is commonly called the auroch. The true auroch is extinct, but the bison resembles him to a great extent. There are only two places on the whole earth where they are found, in Pless and in the hunting preserve of the former Czar in the Bielowicz Forest. The Bielowicz Forest has, of course, suffered tremendously through the war. Many good bison that would otherwise have been shot only by princely personages and the Czar, have been brought down by a musketeer.

May 1917

I arrived at Pless on the afternoon of the twenty-sixth of May and immediately set out from the station. I was impatient to kill a bull that same evening. We travelled along the famous road through the enormous wildlife preserve of the Prince, where formerly many crowned heads had travelled. After about an hour's drive we got out and had to walk for half an hour in order to come to the shooting place. The drivers were already placed waiting for the signal to begin the hunt. I stood on a high point where, the head forester told me, many noblemen had already stood to bag a great number of bison.

May 1917

Overleaf
During summer 1917 the Albatros D.III of Jasta 11 are gathered on the airfield at Roucourt. Note the straight trailing edge to the rudder indicative of an early production model.

"Dear Mamma:

Here I am again and working at top speed. Just now I brought down my number fifty-three. On my return from the base, I stopped at Kreuznach, where I again was invited to lunch with His Majesty, and where I met the King of Bulgaria, who decorated me with the first order of the Cross of Valour. It is worn like the Iron Cross and looks very nice. I was introduced to the Chancellor, Count Dohna, and some other ministers. As regards Oscar, I have only been able to ascertain that he is dead, because he either fell or jumped out of his plane at a height of 1,500 feet. He came down close to the front, but on the other side. By dropping queries over the British lines, I have endeavoured to find out whether his body was recovered. In this respect, the Royal Flying Corps is extremely noble..."

June 18 1917

"Yesterday, Zeumer was killed in air combat. It was perhaps the best that could have happened to him. He knew he had not much longer to live. Such an excellent and noble fellow. How he would have hated to drag himself on toward the inevitable end. For him it would have been tragic. As it is, he died a heroic death before the enemy. Within the next few days, his body will be brought home.

I visited Lothar (at the hospital) and arrived just in time to see him before his removal. He looked tanned and very well, stretched out full length on a divan. He was fully dressed and wore the Pour le Merite around his neck. He is already able to stand and will fully recover. He will be able to walk and ride a horse again, but must have a good long rest."

June 18 1917

By June 1917, the tide of war was gathering momentum. A failed spring offensive on the Aisne led to an Allied plan for a major effort on the British front with the aim of driving the Germans from Belgium and their U-boat bases on the coast. Accordingly, the Messines-Wytschaete ridge had to be taken and to accomplish that some 400 tons of ammonal were placed in tunnels dug deep beneath the German lines. Before dawn on June 7, the entire ridge was blown up, signalling the start of a major effort to push forward. The German Air Service was heavily outnumbered and, pressed by aggressive tactics, faced new challenges that emphasised the expanding gap between new Allied planes and the ageing German designs.

Manfred was recalled from leave tasked with new objectives. He was to organise four Jagdstaffeln into a Jagdgeschwader, or wing, which would operate as a single fighting force. It would render even more applicable the term 'Flying Circus' bestowed by the Royal Flying Corps on von Richthofen's colourful Jasta 11. Its gaily coloured aircraft and the tents used by its personnel as the unit honoured its roving mandate, would make it look for all the world like a travelling fairground. Accordingly, via Supreme Headquarters, von Richthofen was back at Jasta 11 on June 14. Four days later he shot down an R.E.8 flown by Lts. R. W. Ellis and H. C. Barlow.

In a major shift that carried the ground offensive northward, the sector patrolled by Jasta 11 had been largely evacuated and for a while the pilots were hard put to find enemy aircraft. Von Richthofen obtained permission to operate north in the Ypres sector and move the unit from Douai to Marcke. On June 23 while flying his new Albatros D.V (serial number 1177/17) for the first time, von Richthofen shot down a Spad S.7 over Ypres which most probably belonged to a Belgian squadron. There is a possibility, however, that von Richthofen was mistaken in reporting this as a Spad.

Next day, June 24, orders were received forming Jastas 4, 6, 10 and 11 into Jagdgeschwader Nr. 1, and the morning after von Richthofen received orders officially confirming him as commander of J.G.1. With Jasta 11 now at Marcke, Jasta 4 at Cuene, Jasta 6 at Bisseghem and Jasta 10 at Heule, J.G.1 was dispersed around Courtrai. Freedom to select Jasta commanders gave Manfred genuine authority and the opportunity to build an effective and efficient organisation. Not a man for compromise or diplomatic favours, von Richthofen was to command by example and not by encouragement, instantly transferring pilots who failed to meet his own, very high standards. To prevent unnecessary transfers, he chose his men with care.

Clearly, he could not personally run Jasta 11 and J.G.1 while maintaining his presence in the air so he appointed Lt. Kurt Wolff to replace him as head of Jasta 11, Oblt. von Doering to head up Jasta 4, Oblt. von Dostler to run Jasta 6 and Oblt. Ernst Freiherr von Althaus to command Jasta 10. As his adjutant he selected Oblt. Bodenschatz and as technical officer Lt. Krefft. He demanded from his men loyalty to his rules of aerial combat and abstinence from excesses that might impair their performance. A moderate drinker and an occasional smoker, he never indulged in boisterous digressions and frowned upon weaknesses.

On June 25, von Richthofen scored another kill, an R.E.8 flown by Lt. L. S. Bowman and 2nd/Lt. J. E. Power-Clutterbuck, which he attacked with such ferocity that its wings came off while **" the body crashed to the ground between the trenches, burning."** Next day he scored another kill, reportedly an R.E.8 but perhaps a D.H.4, which **"fell with its crew into a hangar between Keibergmelen and Lichtensteinlager, this side of the lines. The aircraft exploded when crashing and destroyed the hangar."** A large amount of administration kept von Richthofen tied up with paperwork and the usual bureaucratic duties military leaders find for their new commanders. But he was determined to maintain his proficiency.

On July 2 von Richthofen attacked another R.E.8 and, again, continued to fire with such incessant fury from a distance of only 150 ft that it **" caught fire and crashed to the ground."** Not unmindful of the need for physical evidence of his kills, von Richthofen had developed an intensity in his attacks that exceeded the necessary damage required to bring the enemy down. From very close range he became increasingly intent on physically breaking up the aircraft under attack by the ferocity of his onslaught, which he achieved by deliberately firing into the wing spars at their root or by 'cutting' the struts with his bullets after making sure the crew were dead or disabled. There was a clinical practicality to this which others, later, would condemn as a bestial killing instinct. The truth was, most probably, much less dramatic.

He had been forced down before by ruptured fuel lines and by a near collapse in the lower wing of his Albatros, but the injury von Richthofen received on July 6, 1917, changed him, said his friends, to a personality he was never to reverse. Jasta 11 took off

“My father makes a distinction between a hunter, a sportsman, and a shooter whose only fun is shooting. Early in the war I found that when I downed an Englishman, my hunting passion was quenched for the time being. I seldom tried to shoot down two Englishmen, one right after another. If one fell, I had the feeling of absolute satisfaction. Only much, much later did I overcome that and also become a shooter.

It was different with my brother. I had an opportunity to observe him when he shot down his fourth and fifth opponents. We attacked a squadron. I was the first to single out an adversary, and my opponent was soon dispatched. Near this Englishman flew a second. Lothar did nothing further to the first, who had not yet fallen and was still in the air. He turned his machine gun on the next one and immediately shot at him after he had barely finished with the other. This one also fell after a short battle.”

1917

Far Right
On July 6, 1917, von Richthofen was shot down and taken to St. Nicholas's hospital at Courtrai. Manfred quickly became frustrated with the boredom of convalescence and was back in action less than three weeks later.

during the morning, the J.G.1 commander at their head, in pursuit of six F.E.2ds from No. 20 Sqdn, RFC. As more German units were drawn up to engage the British planes, four Sopwith Triplanes from No. 10 (Naval) Sqdn, RNAS, joined in until there were reportedly some 40 aircraft milling round. Two F.E.2ds had already been shot down and a third heavily mauled when 2nd/Lt. A. E. Woodbridge in one of the remaining aircraft, piloted by Capt. D. C. Cunnell, fired shots at a red Albatros 1,200 feet away.

It was too far for accuracy but the chance shot that hit von Richthofen came close to killing him, gouging an elongated finger-length groove against his skull and cutting down to the bone. Fortunately, the skull was not shattered. As he was to recall later in vivid detail: *“Suddenly, something strikes me in the head. For a moment, my whole body is paralysed. My arms hang down limply beside me; my legs flop loosely beyond my control. The worst was that a nerve leading to my eyes had been paralysed and I was completely blind. I feel my machine tumbling down - falling. At that moment, the idea struck me, this is how one feels when one is shot down to his death. At any moment I wait for my wings to break off.”*

Unconscious, he was a helpless passenger in the plunging Albatros that would have carried von Richthofen to his death had he not regained the use of his limbs and slowly pulled out of the dive, as he recalled later: *“Soon I regain power over my arms and legs, so that I grip the wheel. Mechanically, I cut off the motor, but what good does that do? One cannot fly without sight. I forced my eyes open - tore off my goggles - but even then I could not see the sun. I was completely blind. The seconds seemed like eternities. I noticed I was still falling. From time to time, my machine had caught itself, but only to slip off again. At the beginning I had been at a height of 12,000 ft, and now I must have fallen at least 6,000 to 9,000 ft. I concentrated all my energy and said to myself, I must see - I must see - I must see.*

“Whether my energy helped me in this case, I do not know. At any rate, suddenly I could discern black-and-white spots, and more and more I regained my eyesight. I looked into the sun - could stare straight into it without having the least pains. It seemed as though I was looking through thick black goggles. First thing I did was to look at the altimeter. I had no idea where I was. Again I caught the machine and brought it into a normal position and continued gliding down. Nothing but shell holes was below me. A big block of forest came before my vision, and I recognized that I was within our lines.

Above

Still wearing a protective head dressing, Manfred allows Lt. Dostler to wear his Pour le Merite after it was announced August 6, 1917, that the latter had been awarded this medal. Dostler was shot down and killed two weeks later.

"First, I wanted to land immediately, for I didn't know how long I could keep up consciousness and my strength; therefore, I went down to 150 ft but could not find amongst the many shell holes a spot for a possible landing. Therefore, I again speeded up the motor and flew to the east at a low height. At this, the beginning, I got on splendidly, but after a few seconds I noticed that my strength was leaving me and that everything was turning black before my eyes. Now it was high time. I landed my machine without any particular difficulties, tore down a few telephone wires, which of course I didn't mind at the moment. I even had enough strength left in me to get up and try to get out of the plane. I tumbled out of the machine and could not rise again - I was weak."

On seeing him spiral toward earth, Lts. Brauneck and Niederhoff swooped down to follow Manfred and circle his aeroplane when it came to rest after landing near La Mortaigne. An officer, Lt. Schroeder, from one of the alert posts watched von Richthofen's fall through a telescope and was quickly on the scene. But Manfred had not lost consciousness and had the sense to refuse alcohol and ask instead for water. As his colleagues patrolled above, protecting events below from the very real threat of strafing from enemy aircraft, frantic efforts were mobilised to get the ace to hospital.

Rushed to St. Nicholas's hospital, Courtrai, at the insistence of an ashen faced patient sporting a hurriedly applied field dressing, Germany's top scoring air ace had escaped death by a whisker. About one-quarter inch separated von Richthofen from his Maker and he was deeply affected by the experience. Never a frivolous or jocular person at best, he would become almost a recluse, ever more intent upon defeating his enemy and intensely persistent in pressing home furious conflict. In the meantime, Oblt. von Doering took over temporary command of J.G.1 and organised revenge the following day, when pilots from Jagdstaffeln 4 and 11 shot down nine aircraft in a frenzied attack on the enemy.

"Dear Mamma:

Many thanks for your dear letter, which gave me great pleasure. I was glad to hear that Lothar is doing well, but he must have a good rest before he takes up his trade again. Physical fitness is its principal requisite. What do you think of our sudden overwhelming successes in the East? Everyone here has been filled with fresh hope. The Russians have made their last ineffective attempts. They should be offered favourable conditions now, and perhaps we could come to an agreement about separate peace. Professor Bush is staying with me, turning out one drawing after another. He is a well-known artist, and has drawn Papa and myself very well indeed. Lothar is the next on his programme. I can walk around now, and will soon go up again."

July 25 1917

CHAPTER EIGHT *Slaughter From The Air*

For nearly three years now, young men had been killing each other along a line dividing Europe from the Swiss mountains to the North Sea. Carnage on a scale unimagined when war began in August 1914 had developed a seemingly unstoppable momentum. New and more fearsome fighting machines had evolved in vain attempts to break the lock of trench warfare. Tanks had been designed and would be first used at the Battle of Cambrai; aircraft had developed into fighting machines capable of combat on a scale impossible three years earlier.

Nowhere was the effect of this horrifying stalemate seen more clearly than in the procession of shattered minds and bodies constantly invalided from the battle fronts to the towns and villages where the flower of a generation had given their lives. If not always in death then certainly through unceasing pain and mental torment. And among the battle hardened warriors, nowhere was it felt more deeply than in the corps of veteran flyers that daily went out to kill in the skies above France and Belgium. The pressure was great and the stress enormous but the gradual erosion of normality in the lives of these very young soldiers took its toll.

Had it not been for his close encounter with death, Manfred von Richthofen would probably not have wearied of this war as soon as he did. Increasingly, he came to hate the business of killing and left testimony to a disillusioned regret over having concentrated too much too quickly in his brief years of

Below
Manfred von Richthofen accompanies General Ludendorff on an inspection of Jasta 11 at Montigny-Ferme on August 19, 1917. Note Manfred's Albatros D.V in the background.

manhood. What had begun as a sport had slowly developed into a chillingly precise and clinical need to kill. There was no longer the thrill of the chase, so enjoyed during the glorious days of Jasta Boelcke. The added responsibilities that came with fame and rank sat uncomfortably on Manfred's shoulders.

Somewhat a loner by nature, Manfred was ill at ease in the presence of generals, field marshalls, emperors and the swooning mass of young women who constantly contrived to be seen with him. Yet he had a sense of humour. When seen in the frequent company of a titled young lady, serving as shorthand-typist as he worked on the draft of his book, Manfred set tongues wagging when he introduced her as his betrothed! The rumour-mongers made much of that, to Manfred's quiet and discreet delight. She was, after all, the daughter of the Duke of Saxe-Coburg-Gotha.

Yet Manfred felt increasingly in need of pursuits and pleasures other men seemed to acquire quite naturally. Probably tone deaf, he could not enjoy music, and he found social gatherings, even among peers, uncomfortable. Manfred was rarely seen in the company of ladies, and had no one particular lady friend. There were many occasions when he was seen dining alone at isolated tables in restaurants.

Manfred von Richthofen was back at the helm of Jagdgeschwader Nr. 1 on July 25, still wearing a partial head dressing and looking slightly overweight; this seemingly unimportant point strangely characterises the victims of shell-shock or deep psychological trauma. But there were new German aircraft to fly and new British planes to fight, and, putting aside his innermost feelings, Manfred was relieved to be actively involved again rather than waiting in hospital for the seemingly endless procession of visitors.

A robust biplane single-seat fighting scout produced by the Royal Aircraft Factory, the S.E.5 had been introduced to the Western Front by the British in April. With some engines, the type was capable of reaching a top speed of more than 130 mph at ground level and of reaching 10,000 feet in 11 minutes. When the diminutive and temperamental Sopwith Camel arrived on the scene during June, it proved in the hands of an experienced pilot to be a devastating killing machine. Highly manoeuvrable, it revealed a ground level top speed in excess of 120 mph and some versions could reach 10,000 feet in less than 9 minutes.

Von Richthofen was not to bag a Sopwith Camel until March 1918, and it was a Nieuport 17 that he claimed as his 58th

66 My dog (Moritz) has one stupid trait. He loves to accompany the planes as they start down the field. Many a flyer's dog, while doing this, has been killed by a propeller. Once Moritz chased after a starting plane, and caught it, unfortunately - and a very beautiful propeller was ruined. Moritz howled terribly, but one of my training failures was made up for in this way. I had always resisted having him clipped, that is, having his ears specially cut. Now the propeller had made up for it on one side. Vanity never bothered him, but the one floppy ear and the other half-clipped do not go well together. In general, if he did not have that defect he would be a handsome hound.99

1917

victory, the first since returning to J.G.1. on August 16. As an acknowledged entry in his victory log it was one of the least well documented and for some reason records of this were removed from the archives. It was the first combat von Richthofen had engaged in since returning to active duty, since his doctors had warned him not to fly. They had good reason, for he found it difficult to fight off nausea and the effects of repeated attempts by doctors to remove small splinters of bone still embedded around the wound. During the fight he nearly became airsick and afterwards exhaustion almost overwhelmed him.

The only post-war indication that this victory took place was in the silver victory cup he ordered from the Berlin jeweller. Now, even the cup has disappeared, but its existence was recorded before Soviet troops overran Schweidnitz toward the end of World War II. This is fortunate for the archivist, because the 60th victory cup, ordered after that victory took place on September 1, was the last one made. Silver was getting scarce in Germany. The effect of the war was taking its toll. Von Richthofen's 59th victory, meanwhile, was recorded on August 26.

August 26th, 1917

7:30 am

Betwen Poelcapelle and Langemarck, this side of the lines.

SPAD One seater, English.

When flying with four of my gentlemen from Jasta 11, I detected at 3,000 metres below me a single SPAD flying above the cloud cover. My adversary was probably trying to find a low-flying German artillery aircraft. I attacked him from out of the sun. He tried to escape by diving, but at this moment I shot at him and he disappeared through the clouds. Following, below the clouds I saw him falling and then explode at a height of 500 metres. The new, very bad F.B. ammunition had done a lot of damage to my aircraft, pressure and intake pipes, etc. If my opponent had only been slightly damaged it would have been impossible for me to have followed as I had to turn in as soon as possible.

Frhr. v. Richthofen
Rittm. and Geschwader Commander

Suffering from the effects of his wound and frustrated by the poor quality of the exploding ammunition which damaged the front end of the Albatros D.V, von Richthofen once more suffered from what was by now clearly a premature return to flying. But there was the need to begin converting from Albatros scouts to the new Fokker triplane, the Dr.I, hurriedly designed when the Sopwith Triplane seemed to be such a great success. The first two Dr.Is arrived at Courtrai on August 21,

" *Dear Mamma:*

I am glad to hear of Lothar's continuing improvement, but under no circumstances should he be allowed to return to the front before he is entirely fit again. If he is permitted to do otherwise, he will suffer a relapse, or he will be shot down. I speak from experience. I have only made two combat fights since my return. Both were successful, but after both of them I was completely exhausted. During the first one, I nearly became air sick. My wound is healing very slowly: It is still as large as a five mark piece. Yesterday they removed another splinter of the bone. I think it will be the last. Some days ago, the Kaiser visited our section to review the troops. We had a rather long conversation. I am scheduled for leave and am looking forward to seeing you all together. **"**

August 28 1917

and on the day von Richthofen secured his 59th victory von Ludendorff came to see the new aircraft for himself. Three days later, Werner Voss flew one bearing the serial 102/17, before taking over his own Dr.I, 103/17. Manfred adopted 102/17 as his own for a while and achieved his next two victories with it:

September 1st. 1917

7.50 am.

Near Zonnebeke, this side of the lines.

Fok F1, No 102 Triplane.

RE 2, English

Flying my triplane for the first time, I attacked with four of my gentlemen a very courageously flown English artillery flyer. I approached and fired 20 shots from a distance of 50 metres, whereupon my adversary fell and crashed near Zonnebeke. Most probably the English pilot took me for an English triplane, as the observer stood upright in the aircraft without thinking of making use of his gun.

Frhr. v. Richthofen
Rittm. and Geschwader Commander

September 3rd. 1917

7.35 am.

South of Bousbecque, this side of the lines.

Inmate: Lieut. A. F. Bird, taken prisoner, unwounded.

Sopwith - 1. Aircraft No: B1795

Engine No: 35123 (80 HP Le Rhone Type 'R').

Machine Gun No: A 4723

Own Aircraft: Fokker F1 102/17 (triplane).

With five aircraft from Staffel 11, I was engaged in a fight with a Sopwith one-seater squadron. At 3,500 metres I attacked one of the enemy's machines. After a while I forced it to land near Bousbecque. I was convinced that I had a very deft opponent, because even at a height of 50 metres he did not surrender, but kept on shooting. Even before landing he fired at our troops and finally smashed his machine, intentionally, against a tree. The Fokker triplane F1 102/17 was undoubtedly better and more reliable than the English machine.

Frhr. v. Richthofen.
Rittm. and Geschwader Commander

Von Richthofen's 60th victory had been an R.E.8 flown by 2nd/Lts. I. B. C. Madge and W. Kember, the former spending the duration of the war in a prison camp, the latter being killed. On his way back from the fight, Manfred hurriedly scribbled three words on a scrap of paper - *My Sixtieth. Manfred* - and dropped it in a small metal cylinder to his father who was now in charge of a reserve battalion nearby. His 61st victim had been a Sopwith Pup piloted by Lt. A. F. Bird who was taken prisoner. With tongue in cheek, von Richthofen attached no fewer than seven affidavits to the request for confirmation, despite the wreckage of the aircraft concerned being available for inspection. It was his way of rebutting criticism that J.G.1 was prone to disregard the strict rules of victory endorsement. It was the last time he was required to submit testimonials!

On September 6, Manfred left on a long overdue period of convalescence and would not fly a Fokker triplane again for more than six months. By that time it was in line for replacement by a biplane, the excellent Fokker D.VII. The myth that von Richthofen flew an aircraft of this type for the

Below
With Anthony Fokker in the cockpit speaking to General von Lossberg while Manfred looks on, the first of two Dr.I triplanes arrived at von Richthofen's J.G.1 on August 21, 1917.

majority of his victories is already self evident. The falsehood is compounded when understanding that not before March 1918 did he fly in combat a triplane which had areas painted in his chosen colour. In fact, he flew an all-red triplane for only 9 of his 80 official victories. But the myth prevails, despite the fact that Manfred was not the best pilot to use the type.

Probably the greatest exponent of the Fokker Dr.I, Werner Voss lived a short and furious life on the type. Coming to Jasta 10 on August 10 with 33 victories to his credit, Voss was a dedicated flyer and found in the Fokker triplane just the right aeroplane for his skills and temperament. Youthful, frivolous and with the same diminutive stature as von Richthofen, Voss shot down 10 aircraft in 21 days beginning September 3. On September 23 he was caught in a fight with some of the best British air aces of World War I and died as he would have wished, furiously blazing away at a swarm of S.E.5a scouts on the day he scored his 48th kill.

Von Richthofen's own triplane (102/17) was destroyed when Kurt Wolff, the Jasta 11 leader, flew the aircraft to his death against Sopwith Camels of No. 10 (Naval) Sqdn, RNAS, on September 15 having scored a total 33 victories since March. The rest of the month and much of October brought little

“Dear Mamma:

I was extremely glad to hear of Lothar's sudden recovery. On my return from leave, we can again go up together and show the English a few tricks. We will be in the same squadron. My bag during the last fortnight has been far from bad - a large elk, three excellent stags, and a buck. I am rather proud of my record, because Papa has only shot three stags in all his life. I am leaving Berlin today and will be with you in less than a week.”

September 30 1917

Above
Standing by the tail of the Sopwith Pup von Richthofen shot down to achieve his 61st official victory, Manfred chats with Lt. Mohnicke.

respite from the tedium of countless patrols with little result and high casualties. All this was veiled from von Richthofen who enjoyed hunting on the estate of the Duke of Saxe-Coburg-Gotha before going on to Adlershof for more consultations about aircraft design. There followed a brief visit to see his mother at Schweidnitz where he put the finishing touches to the book he had started during May.

Von Richthofen was back with J.G.1 on October 23 but there were setbacks ahead. Lt. Heinrich Gontermann was killed when the triplane he was flying (115/17) suffered structural failure and the top wing broke free at 1,500 feet. Two days later Lt. Pastor from Jasta 11 lost his life in another accident caused by structural failure to his Fokker Dr.I (121/17) and the type was grounded. After a quick inspection of the triplanes in their charge, von Richthofen and his technical officer, Lt. Krefft, found numerous examples of shoddy workmanship and construction that had been rushed to hurriedly deliver the aircraft to an unrealistic schedule. By early December structural modifications had been completed at the Fokker works and production of the triplane resumed as the aircraft was returned to flying status; J.G.1 reverted to the type.

By this time the triplane was considered outdated and its replacement, the Fokker D.VII, was already well in hand. Von

Richthofen went back to the Albatros D.V and flew 4693/17 when he claimed a D.H.5 for his 62nd victory on November 23. The only D.H.5 he shot down, there has been conjecture over who was flying the machine that crashed into Bourlon Wood. It was most probably Lt. J. A. V. Boddy of No. 64 Sqdn, RFC. Von Richthofen's next victory was scored a week later against an S.E.5a flown by Capt. P. T. Townsend which he dispatched into a wood near Moevres after firing at it from a range of little more than 300 feet. Once again he was flying an Albatros D.V.

With his score standing at 63, von Richthofen departed on December 12 for a series of technical visits in search of better aircraft. The Fokker triplane had not come up to expectations and although highly manoeuvrable lacked speed and was seriously outdated by more recent Allied types. The Albatros factory had failed to come up with anything radically different to the D.III and D.V which had been designed back in 1916 and although large numbers were still in service it too was seriously outclassed. The selection of new aircraft was an important role for a Geschwaderkommandeur and much depended upon the choices made by aces.

Some notable German pilots gave their approval to certain types of aircraft for small favours from the manufacturers. The company test pilots would prepare the best examples of aircraft on offer and competitions would be held where Army aviators - frequently aces - would fly them and offer their personal opinions on performance, stating their preferences for particular designs. Often the favours heaped on them by the manufacturers amounted to not inconsiderable sums of money. To his credit, perhaps not surprisingly, von Richthofen would have none of that. He knew too well the consequences of endorsing aircraft from slack manufacturers. It could result in the loss of life through poor deisgn. As a front line fighter pilot, he could do little about bad workmanship in the factory but he could avoid patronising the companies that jeopardised the lives of his colleagues.

Richthofen spent his fourth Christmas of the war, mercifully the last for all fighting men, with his unit, his brother and his father. He had mellowed a great deal toward the end of 1917, seeming to abandon the formal relationship he had with fellow officers a year before. Now, he was more casual, seemed less concerned with protocol and became a true leader of men. During this latter period of his short life, after the accident which nearly killed him, von Richthofen became fatalistic and probably had a premonition of his own death. Fellow officers have said that after his accident he could be morose and appeared to believe it

"Dear Mamma:

There is little doing here at present and things are consequently rather dull. I am leaving for Speyer today to look over an aeroplane plant. Christmas I intend spending with my squadron, together with Papa and Lothar. My orderly has already sent a Christmas parcel to Bolko, and I trust I have succeeded in meeting a cadet's tastes."

December 11 1917

Above
Manfred tries out a Pfalz Dr.I triplane during a visit to Speyer in mid-December 1917, finding it lacking in performance compared to the Fokker.

was only a matter of time before he fell victim to some horrible death in the air. Like many of his own victims, he particularly feared being burned alive.

Much was now being demanded of his time and senior officers, Generals and the Kaiser himself urged upon the young captain a caution he was ill prepared to concede. Yet now he mixed his responsibilities as a fighting pilot - no longer the ebullient activity it once had been for him - with his more mundane value as a source of leadership and inspiration. It was as though the mantle of Boelcke, so reluctantly taken up, had now been firmly grasped and von Richthofen became a firm example by which other men tried to fashion their military prowess.

Gone was the arrogance others thought they saw but which had, in fact, been the product of a very particular upbringing. Now he had more time for the casual things of life and yet became ever more serious about the job in hand. There were those around him at the time who began to fear for his life. They saw in him the signs of stress and long term fatigue that presages death, caused by a simple mistake and an error of judgement to which a tired mind so readily succumbs. Especially when gripped by weariness and the loss of purpose that comes from seeing death and destruction on a lavish scale every day for years on end. So it was with Manfred von Richthofen.

CHAPTER NINE *The Last Offensive*

Christmas 1917 came and went and with it another year of war. The experiment which began when Jagdstaffeln 4, 6, 10 and 11 had been grouped into Jagdgeschwader Nr. 1 had proved a great success. Mobile, and with a concentrated force capable of meeting and matching opposition on a large scale, it had been made more effective by an improved alert system which helped vector fighting units to enemy aircraft and concentrations of squadrons protecting reconnaissance and observation units. Comprising Jagdstaffeln 12, 13, 15 and 19, Jagdgeschwader Nr. 2 had been officially formed on August 17, 1917.

Hampered by bad weather and poor visibility, January brought little opportunity for J.G.1 to score. But Manfred was at Brest-Litovsk seeing for himself the ruination of the Romanov dynasty. On a front where he had once plied back and forth in twin-engined bombers he had returned to see a defeated country lay down its arms and take up Bolshevism. Yet even here he found a haven and where once Czar Nicholas II had

"Dear Mamma:

*You will wonder why you have been so long without news from me, but that is always an indication that I am well. In this case, however, I have been seeing much. Lothar has already written you that we were in Brest-Litovsk. There we saw and were introduced to all the prominent diplomats. I should like very much to tell you all about it. As it is, I can only write you that peace was concluded along the lines laid down by Ludendorff. For a few days, we roamed through the forests around Bielowicza, where each of us shot a stag. The stay in the quiet forest has done us both a world of good. I will be in Berlin for a fortnight after the twentieth, when I hope to be able to see you.***"**

January 15 1918

hunted, he went looking for bison and red stag with his brother Lothar with the permission of the new rulers. A class so very different from his own. In cold wintry weather sleighs were transport and the von Richthofens had one of their most enjoyable and relaxed periods together. Entertained by rough peasant stock it was an illuminating experience for the two brothers which Manfred accepted in a way he would have been unable to a year before. For a time the ravages of war were far away.

By January 20 Manfred was in Berlin and Lothar had gone to Schweidnitz to see his mother. The Rittmeister was deeply involved in discussions with the Directorate of Aircraft Production about new aircraft types. At the end of the month a fighter competition would select new models for the Jagdstaffeln. He had hoped to see his mother but duties held him longer than expected and by early February he was back with J.G.1. On the 11th he wrote home apologising for his absence, a hint of melancholy in the opening lines: **"I am sorry that I was kept in Berlin so long that I could not come to Schweidnitz to say good-bye... Now I think I will not come back to Germany for a long, long time. Keep Lothar with you as long as possible..."**

It was not as fatalistic as it might have seemed although he did increasingly act as if in resignation to fate. He knew that Germany was preparing for a major offensive in March that would combine the forces previously occupied on the now quiet Eastern Front, in an effort to overthrow the Allies in the West. J.G.1 would be kept busy trying to seize control of the air and support the ground offensive. It was not clear when he would again have the chance to walk the forests, hunt and visit his mother at Schweidnitz. Also postponed were plans to land at the military school, Wahlstatt, where Bolko von Richthofen was eager to show off his famous elder brother. Manfred deemed the ground too wet and muddy to risk a landing in winter. **"In the autumn, with the crops off the fields, I will do it surely."**

It was March 12, 1918, before von Richthofen scored again. In the previous six months he had shot down just two aircraft, both in one week during November. In the next six weeks he was to increase his official victory score by 17 bringing to 80 the number of formally credited kills. Where previously the majority of his victories had been achieved against two-seat reconnaissance and observation types, 11 of the 17 were single-seat fighting scout biplanes including Sopwith Camels and S.E.5as while 3 of the remaining 6 were Bristol Fighters, now considered a worthy machine to engage.

"Dear Mamma:

I am sorry that I was kept in Berlin so long that I could not come to Schweidnitz to say goodbye. It would have been so pleasant, and I was looking forward to it. Now I think I will not come back to Germany for a long, long time. Keep Lothar with you as long as possible. He is rather negligent with his ears and does nothing to cure them. He loses nothing here. Tell him from me, he should not leave before the first of March. Should things become more lively here, I will advise him by wire. I am afraid Bolko is angry with me, but it was really impossible to make a landing in Wahlstatt. In the autumn, with the crops off the fields, I will do it surely."

February 11 1918

Far Right
Each wearing the Pour le Merite, Manfred and Lothar would score a combined 120 victories before the war's end. Lothar shared with two other pilots ninth position in the list of German air aces.

His first victim of 1918 was a Bristol F.2B flown by Lt. C. F. Clutterbuck and 2nd/Lt. H. J. Sparks from No. 62 Sqdn, RFC. Lothar was with him on patrol when von Ricththofen attacked just after 11:00 am on March 12. Flying the Fokker Dr.1 152/17, **" The aircraft I attacked immediately dived down to 1,000 metres and tried to escape. The observer, who only fired high up in the air, then disappeared into his compartment and only began firing again shortly before the machine landed."** The second victory came a day later when he **" approached to within 20 metres "** of a Sopwith Camel from No. 73 Sqdn, RFC, **" and put holes through his benzine tank."** The pilot, 2nd/Lt. J. M. L. Millett, was killed when his machine caught fire in the air. One of von Richthofen's most detailed combat reports was his 66th victory claim:

March 18th. 1918.
11.15 am.
Above Molain-Vaux road near Andigny.
Sopwith Camel, No 5243, English.
Engine. Clerget No 35751.
Inmates: One Canadian, taken prisoner.

I took off with 30 aircraft of my squadron and flew to the front, commanding all three Staffels at 5,300 metres in height. Just as we were approaching the front, I saw several English squadrons crossing our lines and flying in the direction of Le Cateau. The first squadron we met flew at an altitude of approximately 5,500 metres. I shot with Lieut. Gussman, Staffel 11, at a Bristol Fighter; this was finally destroyed by Lieut. Gussman's guns. Thereupon I took my 30 aircraft in hand, rose to 5,300 metres and pursued two enemy squadrons which had fought their way through to Le Cateau. I attacked just when the enemy turned back and retreated. The enemy machine flying nearest to me, apparently a Breguet or a Bristol Fighter, was attacked by me and Lieut. Lowenhardt of Jasta 10. The tank was shot to pieces and the machine crashed down in a vertical dive. Lieut. Lowenhardt brought down this machine. Then from the centre of two English one-seater squadrons I attacked an aircraft flying pennants and forced it to land near Molain.

Frhr. v. Richthofen.
Rittm. and Geschwader Commander.

The triplane used by von Richthofen for these three victories originally had the standard finish of dark olive upper and pale blue under surfaces. Red fabric covered the upper surface of the top wing, the top and sides of the fuselage and the upper surface of the tailplane as well as both sides of the rudder and wheel covers. Nine of his last fourteen victories were scored in the only all-red triplane he ever flew. By this time, individual colour schemes were a common sight among Jagdstaffeln and there was a prolific array of elaborate markings on German scouts along the Western Front. Given the stiff regulations concerning kill testimonials from fellow pilots, individual markings so easily recognised at a glimpse during combat were a great asset.

The March offensive launched by the Germans in the early morning hours of the 21st was arguably the biggest and most important battle of World War I. With it went the last efforts by Germany to break through the stalemate of trench warfare and immobility. Some 56 divisons had been assembled for the infantry assault and the British were forced to give ground in an ordered retreat. The pilots of J.G.1 were unable to achieve the success they sought because poor weather kept them on the ground for several days. Finally, on the 24th, von Richthofen scored again, **"during a long fight between 10 S.E.5s and 25 machines of my own squadron. Both wings were severed from the English aircraft by my bullets. The remnants were distributed in the area to the west of Combles."**

Next day, **"With five aircraft from Staffel 11 I attacked several English one-seaters north east of Albert. I approached to within 50 metres of one of the enemy's machines and shot at it until it burst into flames. The burning machine fell between Contalmaison and Albert and burnt on the ground. Bombs which had apparently been attached to the aircraft exploded several minutes later."** The day after he got a double within fifteen minutes of each other. The first, at 4:45 pm, was a Sopwith Camel piloted by 2nd/Lt. W. Knox.

"From a distance of not more than the length of an aircraft I shot at him until he burst into flames, this after he had tried to escape by some very deft flying. The machine broke into two parts whilst falling; its body crashed into a small wood near Contalmaison." The second was an R.E.8 flown by 2nd/Lts. V. J. Reading and M. Leggat: **"I dived and placed myself behind it. I fired 100 shots at it and the aircraft caught fire. At first the Englishman defended himself with the observer's gun. The aircraft fell burning and also burnt on the ground."**

Von Richthofen now had 70 confirmed victories to his credit and achieved a triple victory on March 27. His first that day was a Sopwith Camel at low altitude probably out on ground strafing duties. It was brought down from a close distance and with only 150 rounds. Bearing the body of the pilot, Lt. H. W. Ransom, the aircraft slithered **"into a very flooded part of the Ancre."**

"Dear Mamma:

You will have received my wire advising you of Lothar's fall. Thanks to God he is doing nicely. I visit him daily. Please, Mother, don't worry about anything. He is really doing quite well. His nose has already healed, only the jaw is still bad, but he will keep his teeth. Above his right eye he has a rather large hole, but the eye itself has not been damaged. Several blood vessels burst under his right knee and in the left calf. The blood he spat out did not come from any internal injuries. He had merely swallowed some during his fall. He is in the hospital in Cambrai and hopes to be back at the front within a fortnight. His only regret is not to be able to be with us at the present moment."

March 23 1918

Overleaf
Von Richthofen jokes with fellow officers during a visit to Jasta 5 at Boistrancourt early in 1918. The aircraft is a Fokker triplane with the characteristic black and white striping of Jasta 6.

During the afternoon, von Richthofen shot down **" an enemy infantry flyer that was molesting our troops. I managed to approach it, a Bristol Fighter, unnoticed to within 50 metres and succeeded in shooting him down after some 100 shots. The machine fell burning and touched the ground not far from some German columns."** Capts. K. R. Kirkham and J. H. Hedley were taken prisoner.

Five minutes later he saw another Bristol Fighter and **" got on the tail of this machine and shot at it from a distance of 50 metres until it caught fire. I noticed that there was only one inmate; the observer's seat was presumably filled with bombs. I first killed the pilot and then I shot at the aircraft until it broke into pieces. The body of the aircraft fell into the wood burning."** In fact the aircraft had a crew of two, the most likely victims being Capt. H. R. Child and Lt. A. Reeve from No. 11 Sqdn, RFC.

A day later von Richthofen got his 74th victory when he shot down an Armstrong Whitworth F.K.8 flown by 2nd/Lts. J. B. Taylor and E. Betley from No. 82 Sqdn, RFC. **" I recognized an Englishman flying home at an altitude of 500 metres. I approached him having cut off his retreat. After 100 shots the enemy aircraft caught fire. It then crashed down, touched the ground near the wood at Mericourt and kept on burning."** The F.K.8 first appeared in France during January 1917 and was a sturdy and robust two-seat reconnaissance bomber. Well liked by its crew, with a forward firing Vickers and a Lewis for the rear gunner, this was the only F.K.8 shot down by von Richthofen.

Only the day before, an aircraft of this type from No. 2 Sqdn, RFC, had successfully fought off an attack by eight Fokker triplanes. Lt. A. W. Hammond and 2nd/Lt. A. A. McLeod managed to ward off three attackers before the fuel tank started burning. With flames licking over the pilot's cockpit, McLeod climbed out on to the port wing and controlled the aircraft as best he could from that position. He side-slipped the F.K.8 to port, fanning the flames away from the observer who, although wounded, kept up a spirited return fire. Hammond had a serious problem in that the bottom of his cockpit had fallen out and he had to use his elbows to hold himself in the aircraft. Wounded five times, McLeod managed to get the machine down on the ground and then help Hammond from the rear cockpit. For this remarkable feat, McLeod was awarded the Victoria Cross on May 1. Such was the spirit of von Richthofen's opponents.

Von Richthofen was getting weary of the intense action as the confirmed victory scores were merely the tip of a major effort to

" Hanging from the ceiling in my dugout is a lamp I had made, as a conversation piece, from the engine of a plane I shot down. I mounted small lamps in the cylinders, and this chandelier looks fantastic and weird. When I lie that way, I have much to think about. I write this without knowing if anyone except my closest relatives will ever see it.

The battle now taking place on all fronts has become awfully serious; there is nothing left of the 'lively, merry war' as our deeds were called in the beginning. Now we must fight off despair and arm ourselves so that the enemy will not penetrate our country. I now have the greatest feeling that people have been exposed to quite another Richthofen than I really am."

March 1918

find and defeat the enemy in the air. Frequently, J.G.1 flew more than 100 sorties a day which meant every pilot getting in between two and four flights between dawn and dusk. A concerted effort at the end of March brought little success as poor flying conditions once again prevented the Flying Circus from achieving the desired quota of sorties. On April 1, the British merged the Royal Flying Corps and the Royal Naval Air Service to form the Royal Air Force. A day later, J.G.1 took up a forward flying field at Harbonnieres south-west of Lechelle, the most south-westerly position they were to occupy.

Just after noon on April 2, von Richthofen was flying his all-red triplane 477/17 when **I attacked an English RE. As my adversary only saw me very late I managed to approach to within 50 metres. From 10 metres distance I shot at him until he began to burn. When the flames appeared I could see how the pilot and the observer were leaning out of their aircraft to escape the flames. The machine did not explode in the air but gradually went down burning. It fell uncontrolled to the ground where it exploded and burnt to ashes.** So died 2nd/Lts. E. D. Jones and R. F. Newton in R.E.8 A3868 from No. 52 Sqdn, RAF. It made a grim sight.

Over the next several days J.G.1 personnel came and went. A recent recruit, and a rising star with 22 victories to his credit, Ernst Udet was admitted to a local hospital with earache. And another von Richthofen, Manfred's cousin Wolfram, joined the Flying Circus. Rain and wind kept the flyers grounded until April 6 when J.G.1 accounted for nine Sopwith Camels and a Bristol Fighter, Manfred getting his 76th victory. Flown by Capt. S. P. Smith of No. 46 Sqdn, RAF, **The English aircraft which I attacked started to burn after only a few shots from my guns. Then it crashed to the ground, burning, near the little wood north east of Villers Bretonneaux, where it kept burning.** Again, Manfred was close enough to observe the grisly detail.

Next day, the 7th, von Richthofen scored another double victory although each has its own mystery. At 11:30 in the morning **With four machines of Staffel 11 I attacked several S.E.5s near Hangard. I shot at an enemy aircraft some 200 metres away. After I had discharged 100 shots the enemy aircraft broke into pieces.** This was an unusually long range for von Richthofen to open fire and some have considered the possibility that the S.E.5 was destroyed by a chance hit from a field gun. Observers said the aircraft suddenly blew apart and drifted down in small fragments. Some sources have said the victim was Capt. G. B. Moore but he was not killed until the following day, at the same time but far to the north of where von Richthofen was flying.

When I read my book, I smile at the insolence of it. I now no longer possess such an insolent spirit. It is not because I am afraid, though one day death may be hard on my heels; no, it's not that reason, although I think enough about it. One of my superiors advised me to give up flying, saying it will catch up with me one day.

But I would become miserable if now, honoured with glory and decorations, I became a pensioner of my own dignity in order to preserve my precious life for the nation while every poor fellow in the trenches endures his duty exactly as I did mine.

I am in wretched spirits after every aerial battle. But that no doubt is an after-effect of my head wound. When I set foot on the ground again at my airfield after a flight, I go to my quarters and do not want to see anyone or hear anything. I think of this war as it really is, not as people at home imagine, with a Hoorah! and a roar. It is very serious, very grim...

March 1918

Just over 30 minutes later, at 12:05 pm, **''I was observing a chain of German aircraft pursuing an English aircraft when they were attacked from the rear. I dashed to their assistance and attacked an English aircraft. After putting myself behind him several times, my adversary fell.''** Claiming a Spad single-seat scout, von Richthofen was credited with his 78th victory. But there were no French Spads lost that day and the only British aircraft that fell on April 7 was a Nieuport 27 during the late evening. His two victories on this day, precisely two weeks before his death, are shrouded in mystery and we may never know the truth.

Far Left
Posing in front of a Fokker triplane, Manfred and Lothar von Richthofen show and off two different sets of flying clothing. Not all German pilots got to wear fur!

CHAPTER TEN *The Last Chase*

The German lines had been pushed far to the south-west of their original positions before the March offensive and a great bulge of newly occupied German territory extended from Arras almost as far as Amiens. J.G.1 was given order after order, each countermanded by another directive which did nothing but confuse the Jagdstaffeln commanders and frustrate efforts at concentrating on the air war. Rain, cloud, early morning mist, all played their part in the wearisome business of juggling priorities and operational necessities. Finally, a move to Cappy was approved and von Richthofen gave orders for the Flying Circus to roll.

It was a depressing location. Situated on the Somme valley the place was damp, bleak, and twelve miles from the nearest town of significance. Years of war had pulverised the landscape and a pall of death hung in the air. Pockmarked like a desolate moonscape with craters and littered with the wreckage of incessant bombardment, Cappy was seemingly removed from the rest of the world, a place waiting for the dead and the dying.

Many would testify later that they felt a chilling sense of foreboding when they turned up in the trucks and motorised waggons with tents and trappings and all the many items essential to keep aircraft in a flying condition.

It took several days to get the place operational and then more rain threatened to turn the 'airfield' into a quagmire. Endless administrative duties kept von Richthofen at his makeshift desk, filling in forms, clearing the latest staff changes and approving rosters for duty. April 20 dawned dank and inhospitable. In three days he would escape this gloomy place and pay a visit, with Joachim Wolff, to the Voss hunting estates at the invitation of the late Werner Voss's father. It had rained spasmodically throughout the day, splatters of rain that turned puddles into sheets of water, the sky overhung with brooding cloud. But still there was an opportunity to go aloft and search for prey.

It was early evening in clearing weather, that von Richthofen took off with six of his fellow pilots from Jagdstaffel 11. They headed toward the lines but soon a flight of Camels came into view led by Capt. D. Bell from No. 3 Sqdn, RAF. Their commanding officer, Maj. Raymond-Barker was part of the flight and along with the rest responded to a signal from Bell to wheel around and face the triplanes. As they came through, von Richthofen flicked his triplane (425/17 which he was flying for the first time) on to the tail of Sopwith Camel D6439 flown by Raymond-Barker and sent it burning to the ground.

Wheeling back around to rejoin the main fight von Richthofen attached himself to the tail of Sopwith Camel B7393 piloted by 2nd/Lt. D. G. Lewis, who tried everything he knew to shake off the Red Baron. Almost all red, his triplane had been spotted by Lewis, who thus knew the identity of his attacker. Closing up fast and tucking in tight, von Richthofen poured a succession of hot lead into the British scout and lit its petrol tank until the Camel became an inferno destined to crash to earth only yards away from where Maj. Raymond-Barker's Camel lay burning on the ground. Lewis struggled from the wreckage but was unable to save Raymond-Barker. Later that evening, Manfred von Richthofen wrote his last two combat reports:

April 20th. 1918.

6.40 pm.

South west of Bois de Hamel.

Sopwith Camel: Englishman.

Fok Dr.1 No 425/17, painted red.

Enemy aircraft burnt.

With six aircraft of Staffel 11 I attacked a large enemy squadron. During the fight I observed that a triplane was being attacked and shot at from below by a Camel. I put myself behind the enemy and brought him down, burning, with only a few shots. The enemy aircraft dashed down near the forest of Hamel where it burned further on the ground.

Frhr. v. Richthofen.
Rittm. and Geschwader Commander.

April 20th. 1918.

6.43 pm.

North east of Villers Bretonneux.

Sopwith Camel: Englishman.

Fok Dr.1 No 425/17, painted red.

Enemy aircraft burnt.

Three minutes after I had brought down the first machine I attacked a second Camel of the same enemy squadron. My adversary dived, caught his machine and repeated this manoeuvre several times. I approached him as near as possible when fighting and fired 50 shots until the machine began to burn. The body of the machine burnt in the air, the remnants dashed to the ground north east of Villers Bretonneux.

Frhr. v. Richthofen.
Rittm. and Geschwader Commander.

A lone Fokker triplane followed Lewis's Camel to the ground and flew low over the wreckage. It may have been von Richthofen. If it was, he was gazing for the last time at victims he had subdued with his powerful talent for sending aircraft to destruction and airmen to their doom. He had no reason to doubt that after two more days spent increasing his score he would have the welcome relaxation of the Voss estates, no sense of impending death.

Next morning, Sunday April 21, dawn crept slowly upon the grey sheds and tarpaulins of J.G.1 as the weather gave promise of some sorties. There had been a general improvement in weather conditions over the last three days. Flying had been almost impossible on the 19th but an evening sortie had at last been possible on the previous day. With their flying clothes donned and some, including von Richthofen, wearing parachute harnesses the pilots waited for orders to take off. For a while they sported in mock play and Manfred seemed relaxed and at ease. Perhaps the thought of a much needed rest had quelled the foreboding of preceding weeks.

Above
Incorrectly published on many occasions purporting to be the last shot taken of von Richthofen, the German ace plays with his dog Moritz early in 1918 with a Fokker Dr. I in the background sporting the pre-March national markings.

❝ The most beautiful creature ever created is my elm coloured Great Dane, my 'little lap dog' - Moritz. I bought him for five Marks from a nice Belgian in Ostend. The mother was a beautiful animal, as was his sire; he was therefore quite pure bred. I am convinced of that. Zeumer took a second one and called him 'Max.' Max came to a sudden end under a car, but Moritz thrived splendidly. He slept in bed with me and was very well trained. Ever since Ostend he had accompanied me step by step and had grown in my affection. From month to month Moritz got bigger and bigger, and gradually my tender little lap dog developed into quite an enormous animal. ❞

1917

It was time to fly and the adjutant, Karl Bodenschatz, passed word for the triplanes to take off. They left in two flights, the first comprising von Richthofen, his cousin Wolfram and Vizefeldwebel Scholz, and the second Lts. Weiss, Wenzl and Karjus. Minutes later they had gathered into formation and moved toward the sector they were assigned to patrol. They were to search for British observation aircraft in attempts to prevent them spying on activities preceding a new push. It would have been relatively easy pickings for the triplane pilots if that was all they would encounter on that routine April morning. But it was not.

Delayed more than an hour by bad visibility and mist, a flight of Sopwith Camels from No. 209 Sqdn, RAF, finally took to the air at 9:35 am and moved toward their patrol sector between Hangard and Albert. Led by Capt. A. R. Brown the flight included Lts. Lomas, Mellersh, Mackenzie and May, a newcomer making his first offensive patrol and who had been cautioned to watch out for the enemy and not to get drawn into dog-fights. At five minute intervals two more flights led by Capts. A. W. Redgate and Capt. Le Boutillier departed. By 9:45 am all fifteen aircraft were airborne and flying on a line tangent to the patrol being flown by von Richthofen and his five fellow pilots.

At 10:25 am Le Boutillier's flight spotted two Albatros biplanes carrying out a reconnaissance for the German 12th Army. They swooped down to attack, Lt. Taylor shooting down one and scaring off the other. While the flight went searching for the remaining Albatros, Brown's leading flight had reached the southernmost point of their patrol area and turned back to retrace their outward leg. They saw the engagement and flew on toward the Somme in a north-easterly direction. Meanwhile, von Richthofen's patrol had met up with Jasta 5 flying east to west along the Somme valley. By this time, Lt. Joachim Wolff had taken off to join von Richthofen and two of the original six transferred to the Jasta 5 patrol by prior arrangement, leaving five in the group led by Manfred von Richthofen.

Because the two converging British and German patrols were at different heights, and because there was a considerable amount of cloud around at altitude and mist along the Somme river, they were unlikely to see each other. However, two R.E.8s from No. 3 Sqdn, Australian Flying Corps, on observation at 7,000 feet were attacked by four triplanes from Jasta 5, one of which was shot down. As the remaining triplanes struggled to regain the patrol they drifted over the British lines. The resulting anti-aircraft bursts got the attention of Capt. Brown. He turned in their direction, waggled his wings for three others in his flight to follow, leaving May to observe the ensuing scrap. They dived down from 12,000 feet, just as von Richthofen's flight turned toward the Camels.

The separated triplanes were between Brown's flight and von Richthofen's group. These were engaged first and Mellersh shot down one with a blue tail but within a minute or so von Richthofen's flight was in the fray. Up above, May was tempted beyond caution and shot at a passing triplane flown by Wolfram von Richthofen. Soon, he was in the thick of the fight and losing altitude, outclassed and soon disarmed as his twin Vickers guns jammed because he kept them open too long. Deciding to extricate himself just as quickly as possible, May fell away and headed for the Somme valley.

Von Richthofen had seen the tell-tale signs of a novice and darted quickly on to May's tail, driving him further down until they were only a few hundred feet above the Somme, flying west along its northern bank. The main fray had been directly over the Somme on a line between Le Hamel and Sailley-le-Sec but now the hunter and the hunted were locked in a race to the death. Brown saw this and realising May stood no chance against an experienced pilot dived from 3,000 feet to May's rescue as quickly as he could. Von Richthofen was certain of victory but his victim was so inexperienced it was difficult predicting what he would do next.

Twisting and turning, throwing his Camel every way possible but slowing in the process, May had von Richthofen getting closer by the second. Manfred reached down, loosened his shoulder straps to allow free movement and crouched forward toward the butts of twin Spandau machine guns set in the top decking of the fuselage directly in front of the cockpit, his steely eyes focused along the sights. Blips of gunfire poked and prodded May's Camel, taunting him and probing for a clear line of fire. But May did none of the predictable things, frustrating von Richthofen who refused to let go. Clearly this was not a victim worthy of his skills but the German ace would not give up.

Rapidly overhauling the triplane and pursued Camel as he dived upon von Richthofen from behind and above, Brown got in a quick burst about a half-mile before all three would pass Vaux-sur-Somme which lay to their right. Brown's hectic dive gave him a speed advantage of about 40 mph as he rushed to within two lengths of the Fokker, 150 ft above the right bank of the Somme. Tracers whizzing past the triplane alerted von Richthofen to this surprise attack. He flinched, shot a backward glance at Brown as the Camel overhauled the triplane and climbed away to the left in the general direction of Corbie, then resumed his concentration on May's Camel.

Later, Brown would testify that this was the moment he saw von Richthofen jerk his body to one side and slump forward. What Brown saw in fact was Manfred's momentary reaction to the burst of fire from the Camel's machine guns before von Richthofen resumed his crouched position intent on the target ahead. As Brown climbed away to the left of the flight path taken by von Richthofen and May his starboard wings obscured the view of what happened next. But others had a clearer view of the whole scene in better perspective than the participants.

High above, some of the original formation could see what was going on across the lines. Capt. Le Boutillier watched Brown dive down and hit the triplane with tracer before sweeping into a climb, expending forward momentum from the dive. Higher still, Joachim Wolff saw von Richthofen's red coloured triplane charging after the novice Camel pilot now penetrating behind the British lines. He wondered why von Richthofen should so blatantly contravene his own rules by pressing on down to ground level and penetrating the British defences, thereby exposing himself to ground fire.

Now west of Vaux-sur-Somme, the chase was down to between 60 feet and 100 feet and von Richthofen was only 150 feet behind the Camel, twisting, turning and trying to mirror every chaotic move it made to escape. They were now about two miles behind the lines and flying deeper into British held territory, getting lower all the time. It made no sense. Von Richthofen was risking his life with ever increasing certainty of death and fate was about to level the odds. Flying parallel to the Somme the two aircraft came upon rising ground along the north bank of the river. A cluster of machine gun positions was spread across the whole area and the two aircraft were now well within range of the 53rd Battery, Australian Field Artillery.

Situated on the rise, Sgt. C. D. Popkin and Private R. F. Weston manned a Vickers and could clearly see the Camel and its pursuer coming directly at them from the direction of Vaux. The planes turned to the left of their position and were so close that Popkin had to wait for May's Camel to sweep past before he opened up a seven second burst with his Vickers gun. Both aircraft were now so low that they were rising and falling with every dip and rise in the ground. When Popkin fired Weston thought the triplane faltered and wobbled. But still it hung tenaciously to May's tail, refusing to loosen its grip on the fleeing Camel.

High up on the ridge to the north-west of the Somme, Ray McDiarmid and Joe Hill of the 8th Brigade looked across and saw the dash up the valley as first the Camel then the triplane flew directly between the positions of Gunner Robert Buie, to their immediate left, and Gunner William Evans, farther off to their right. The two aircraft flew almost directly over Buie's position. Both Buie and Sapper Tom Lovell standing alongside saw von Richthofen glancing around, his triplane hard on the Camel's tail. But they could not fire for fear of hitting May. They did, however, see von Richthofen firing at May in short bursts and bullets sprayed the earth on the side of the ridge, hitting pots and pans with resounding clangs.

Then Evans fired, paused, and Buie opened up when the triplane had gone through Evans' position giving him a clear field of view. As Buie fired, splinters flew off the triplane, which jerked and banked hard seemingly to avoid the fire. Evans fired

Apart from us five, there was Staffel No. 5, not far from us over Sailley-le-Sec. Above us were more Sopwith Camels, seven in all, but they partly attacked No. 5 Staffel, and some remained high in the air. One or two, however, came down on us. We started to fight immediately. During the fight, I saw the captain (Manfred von Richthofen) several times not far off but as yet I had seen him bring down no plane.

Of our special group, only Lt. Karjus was with me. Scholz was fighting somewhere over Sailley-le-Sec, and Lt. von Richthofen was, as a beginner, not quite up to the affair. While I and Karjus are fighting two or three Camels, I see that the captain's red machine is engaging a Camel which, apparently hit, drops down and then retreats to the west. This took place on the other side of Hamel.

We had a violent east wind, and most probably the captain had forgotten this fact. As soon as I had more freedom in the fight, I took good aim and brought down my Camel. While it was dashing down, I looked for the captain and spotted him at a very low height somewhere over the Somme and not far from Corbie. He was still pursuing the Camel.

I shook my head involuntarily and wondered why the captain was following a machine so far behind the enemy lines. Just as I am looking to see where my victim is going to crash on the ground I hear machine gun fire behind me. A new Camel is attacking me. He puts twenty holes into my plane.

After getting rid of him, I look for the captain, but the only one I can see is Karjus. It was then I felt the first fore-bodings of disaster, because I ought to have seen him, provided all had gone well. We flew in circles, were attacked once by an Englishman whom we chased as far as Corbie, but of the captain we saw nothing whatsoever. We returned, anxious and nervous. Lt. Joachim Wolff

April 24 1918

again and had a direct line of sight into the triplane's cockpit as it turned to its right. At the first shots Manfred's head jerked and reaching for his face he tore the goggles from his eyes and threw them out. He had done this before, when so narrowly cheating death on July 6, 1917. For a second or two the engine throttled up to maximum revs, then died down, and the sound was replaced by the rush of air through three red wings.

The triplane wobbled, side-slipped and wallowed around losing height. It had slowed appreciably to near stalling speed as it slid jerkily toward the ground. Sgt. Popkin got another clear view as it turned north-east seeming to begin a spiral to the right, then a drift to the left, opening fire for a few seconds as it seemed to be turning to attack the gunners. About half a mile to the west, Brown's Camel appeared and its pilot got a clear view of the doomed triplane. Thinking it to have been the consequence of his earlier attack, he later claimed von Richthofen as his victim.

Within seconds the triplane dropped to the beet field alongside the Bray-Corbie road, the undercarriage breaking after the aircraft bounced more than 10 feet into the air and fell back to the ground. It slewed round, one blade of the two-bladed propeller having splintered, to face the Bray-Corbie road. Von Richthofen had been thrown forward, smashing his face into the butts of the twin Spandau machine guns. But who fired the shot that killed von Richthofen?

Was it Evans or Buie with their machine guns on the ground? Clearly, Brown could not have done it. The evidence refutes his claim, despite its being upheld by many credible sources. Or was it, as some believe, an unknown Australian soldier with a rifle among a platoon of 21 manning a reserve trench nearby under the authority of Lt. Wood? They were in exactly the right spot to get a perfect line of sight. Alerted by machine gun fire, von Richthofen's sudden banking manoeuvre would have exposed him to a single bullet from a rifleman in that trench.

The triplane came to rest shortly before 10:50 am, nose down and tilted to the left. The pilot was dead, his neck ringed with bruises caused by the violent jerking motion of his head thrust first forward then back without restraint when the triplane crash landed. Or, perhaps, by the silken cord around his neck holding the small binoculars tucked in the front of his flying jacket. Alongside the red aeroplane lay Manfred's fur hat, thrown clear at last motion. On the side of the cockpit rested his head, his body slumped and only partly restrained by the loosened harness. His nose was broken and his lip cut. He was thoroughly soaked in blood from the torso down. His hand held the triplane's control column in a death-grip difficult to open.

In the interval between being first hit and crash landing, von Richthofen had probably cut off his engine, after first opening the throttle perhaps to fly out of the ground fire, causing a brief burst of power. Examination of the engine shows that it was stationary when the triplane hit the ground. Within minutes a group of Australian gunners had converged at the scene. Within hours, General Rawlinson commanding the British Fourth Army, had a team of officers on hand to investigate the incident. Meanwhile, a salvage party went out to retrieve the body and the triplane - or what was left of it after the souvenir hunters had finished picking it over.

Von Richthofen's body was given two cursory medical examinations, the first at 11:30 pm on the 21st and the second mid-morning next day. No post mortem was carried out. General Sir Henry Rawlinson, friend of Winston S. Churchill and a man of independent viewpoints, was in no doubt about the evidence. In his view it credited Gunners Buie and Evans with shooting down von Richthofen. He sent them a congratulatory message thanking them for their effort. But the RAF would not accept this and insisted that Brown had shot him down. They drew comfort from the evidence of the medical report prepared at their insistence. It refers to a single wound passing from right to left, entering the torso just in front of the right arm pit and exiting one-half inch above the left nipple having been deflected forward after striking the spine.

This, it was said, was the evidence that Brown killed von Richthofen as the latter twisted round exposing his right side so that the bullet could enter the torso. What was discounted by the medical officers was that the bullet had entered from the right but from a slightly forward angle. Exactly the angle matching the line of fire from Evans' machine gun or a rifleman in the reserve trench. Also, some witnesses believe von Richthofen had other wounds not referred to by the RAF.

Several Australians at the crash site testified that he had wounds in his legs and abdomen through which he had lost a considerable quantity of blood. They appeared to have been inflicted from the front and slightly below and could not have been caused by Brown. If there were abdominal wounds they may have been caused by Buie's gun while the trunk wound most likely came from Evans' brief burst, or a rifleman, when von Richthofen banked in reaction to the ground fire.

In any event, would a machine gun not have left more evidence of multiple hits? The large amount of blood in the abdominal area may have pooled there from the bullet wound, and may not have been from additional wounds some witnesses thought they saw. In which case von Richthofen's initial, jerky reaction in the air may have been due solely to the surprise of bullets whistling round his ears seconds before a rifleman found his target. We will probably never know for sure.

So died Manfred von Richthofen, who in death as well as life was surrounded by myth and legend. As a warrior he was respected by his foe and an effort was made to give him a decent burial. A little after 4:00 pm on April 22, he was taken on a Crossley tender to a small cemetery at Bertangles. Inside its rusting gate a fresh grave had been dug. Surrounding it, grim faced, stood officers with magnificent wreaths at hand. In quiet observation, the local community - men, women, boys and girls - stood a silent brooding vigil on the ceremony. For some unknown reason his body was laid to rest feet nearest the cross, which had been hurriedly fashioned that morning.

It was a grim little place, as those who were there remembered. The trees were stark and the ground was rough and uneven, the cemetery unkempt. After a brief service by an Anglican chaplain, twelve rifles fired three times in salute and the burial party withdrew. That night the villagers tore down the cross, made from a four-bladed propeller with three blades trimmed close to the hub and surmounted by an inscribed aluminium plate. They also destroyed the flowers and tried to dig up the body with their hands, so incensed were they at this German laid to rest in their cemetery.

When all the evidence is read the logical conclusion is that Manfred von Richthofen was killed by ground fire, from either the bullets fired by Australian Gunners Buie and Evans or an unknown rifleman in the reserve trench. By pursuing an enemy to ground level across enemy held territory von Richthofen exposed himself to an inevitable and predictable end. He made the ultimate error of judgement and paid the supreme price, sacrificing his life in a worthless chase against a novice fleeing for his life. In the end, ever the hunter, he could not give up the pursuit of victory and died probably as he would have wished - tenaciously pursuing the enemy of his beloved Fatherland.

The news of Manfred von Richthofen's death came slowly to his fellow officers at Jagdgeschwader Nr.1 when first they were told by telephone that he had been seen alighting on a hill north of Corbie on the British side of the lines. Confirmation of their worst fears was delivered late on the evening of the 22nd, the day after he died. RAF pilots dropped cannisters carrying the message 'Rittmeister von Richthofen was fatally wounded in aerial combat and was buried with full military honours.' Nine days later his mother, his father, Lothar, Bolko and his sister Ilse were at home together in Schweidnitz for what would have been his 26th birthday.

Meanwhile, at J.G.1 the adjutant, Karl Bodenschatz handed Oblt. Wilhelm Reinhard a small envelope which carried the following message dated March 10, 1918: **❝ In the event that I do not return from a patrol, Oberleutnant Reinhard of Jasta 6 is to command the Geschwader.❞** And it was signed, **❝ Freiherr von Richthofen, Rittmeister.❞** So it was that Wilhelm Reinhard took up the mantle of Germany's highest scoring air ace of World War I, but only for just over two months. On July 3, he was killed flying a new aircraft in tests at Adlershof and a new master of J.G.1 was approved three days later. His name was Hermann Goering and he would score 22 victories, although his later exploits would bring him greater fame.

Shortly after the war Manfred's remains were moved to a cemetery at Fricourt where thousands more were buried. On November 15, 1925, his brother Bolko presided over the removal of his body from Fricourt via Albert and Strasbourg to Berlin. Along the way thousands of patriotic Germans witnessed the solemn processional transfer of his remains from a foreign land to German soil. British and American dignatories were in attendance at a special state service on November 20 when Field Marshal von Hindenburg, preceded only by Manfred's mother and Bolko, led the rest of his family and members of J.G.1 to Manfred von Richthofen's final resting place at Invaliden Cemetery.

A year later his mother unveiled a flat memorial stone but in 1938 Hermann Goering laid a fine monumental surround on the grave. Manfred's father had died in 1920 and Lothar had been killed in an aeroplane accident in 1922. His mother and Ilse fled Schweidnitz one cold wintry night in January 1945, with the Russian Army at their heels, leaving all Manfred's trophies and personal possessions. They have been lost, probably for ever. Baroness Kunigunde von Richthofen died in the early 1960s followed by Bolko in 1971.

Manfred Freiherr von Richthofen was one of the last truly great Prussian aristocrats that saw a world he was bred to love crumbling all around him. It was ironic that one of the last places he was to visit away from the Western Front brought him face to face with Bolsheviks who, as Soviets in another war, would pillage and destroy all the places he loved best. Yet today, he is still an enigma, his diaries giving glimpses of compassion and a reflective nature he hid. He was, in the final analysis,

❝ Richthofen is dead. All airmen will be pleased to hear that he has been put out of action, but there will be no one amongst them who will not regret the death of such a courageous nobleman.

Several days ago, a banquet was held in honour of one of our 'aces'. In answering the speech made in his honour, he toasted Richthofen, and there was no one who refused to join. Thus Englishmen honoured a brave enemy.

Both airmen are now dead; our celebrated pilot had expressed the hope that he and Richthofen would survive the war so as to exchange experiences in times of peace.

Anybody would have been proud to have killed Richthofen in action, but every member of the Royal Flying Corps would also have been proud to shake his hand had he fallen into captivity alive.❞

April 24 1918   AEROPLANE

merely a product of his age and a man of his time. But that age has gone and times have changed. In the words of a compassionate obituary written in an English aviation journal shortly after he had been shot down:

'Manfred von Richthofen is dead. He was a brave man, a clean fighter and an aristocrat. May he rest in peace.'

Below
This photograph, showing wreaths and floral tributes from the Royal Flying Corps and others, was dropped behind the German lines after von Richthofen's funeral at Bertangles.

CHAPTER ELEVEN *Technical Details*

Technical details of the
fighting machines flown by
Manfred von Richthofen and a full
log of all his victories.

*"Among the chief properties of a good
fighter plane are the following: A good plane
must lose altitude when curving and after
flying and turning several times on its back,
provided of course, the motor is doing full
speed. It would be ideal if a plane could
even gain in altitude while performing these
manoeuvres, but this is not the case with the
Albatros D.III, and that is its chief
drawback.*

*When moving the side or altitude rudders,
even the slightest change must effect a big
movement. With the Albatros, the ailerons
are not quite sufficient, and this is a most
important factor with a fighter plane. Great
speed and great altitude are both necessary.
To be able to fly slowly by regulating the
motor is very essential. A fighter plane must
be able to stand the strain of diving down
3,000 ft. The Albatros does not always do
this."* **MANFRED FREIHERR VON RICHTHOFEN 1917**

DATE	TIME	LOCATION	AIRCRAFT	SQUADRON	VICTORY NO.	OFFICIAL SCORE	PILOT	OBSERVER	NO.
1915 Sept		Champagne	Farman S.11	French	1				1
1916 Apr 25		Douaumont	Nieuport 11	French	2				2
1916 Sept 17	11:00	Villers Plouich	F.E.2b (7018)	No. 11 RFC	3	1	2nd/Lt. L. B. F. Morris (died)	Lt. T. Rees (died)	3
1916 Sept 23	11:00	Beugny	Martinsyde G.100	No. 27 RFC	4	2	Sgt. H. Bellerby (died)		
1916 Sept 30	11:50	Fremicourt	F.E.2b	No.11 RFC	5	3	Lt. F. C. Lansdale (killed)	Sgt. Clarkson (killed)	
1916 Oct 7	09:10	Equancourt	B.E.12 (6618)	RFC	6	4	2nd/Lt. W. C. Fenwick (killed)		
1916 Oct 10	18:00	Boeux. Arras	B.E.12	RFC	7	5	S. Cookerell		
1916 Oct 16	17:00	Ypres	B.E.12 (6580)	RFC	8	6	Lt. C. R. Tidsdale		
1916 Oct 25	09:35	Bapaume	B.E.12 (6629)	No. 21 RFC	9	6A	2nd/Lt. A. J. Fisher (wounded)		4
1916 Nov 3	14:10	Loupart Wood	F.E.2b (7010)	RFC	10	7	Sgt. G. C. Baldwin (killed)	2nd/Lt. C. A. Bentham (killed)	
1916 Nov 9	10:30	Beugny	B.E.2c (2506)	RFC	11	8	Lt. G. F. Knight (died)	2nd/Lt. J. G. Cameron (killed)	
1916 Nov 20	09:40	Gueudecourt	B.E.12	RFC	12	9	Unidentified		
1916 Nov 20	16:15	Gueudecourt	F.E.2b (4848)	No. 22 RFC	13	10	Lt. G. Doughty (killed)	2nd/Lt. G. Stall (wd; p.o.w.)	
1916 Nov 23	15:00	Bapaume	D.H.2 (5964)	No. 24 RFC	14	11	Maj. L. G. Hawker (killed)		
1916 Dec 11	11:55	Mecatel	D.H.2 (5986)	No. 32 RFC	15	12	Lt. P. B. G. Hunt (wd; p.o.w.)		
1916 Dec 20	11:30	Monchy-le-Preux	D.H.2 (7927)	No. 29 RFC	16	13	Lt. A. G. Knight (killed)		
1916 Dec 20	13:45	Noreuil	F.E.2b (A5446)	No. 18 RFC	17	14	Lt. L. G. D'Arcy (killed)	Sub/Lt. R. C. Whiteside (killed)	
1916 Dec 27	16:25	Ficheux, Arras	F.E.2b (6997)	RFC	18	15	Unidentified	Unidentified	
1917 Jan 4	16:15	Metz-en-Couture	Sopwith Pup (N5193)	No. 8 RNAS	19	16	Flt/Lt. A. S. Todd (killed)		
1917 Jan 23	16:10	Lens	F.E.8	No. 40 RFC	20	17	2nd/Lt. J. Hay (killed)		
1917 Jan 24	12:15	Vitry	F.E.2b (6937)	No. 25 RFC	21	18	Capt. O. Greig (wd; p.o.w.)	Lt. J. E. MacLenan (wd; p.o.w.)	
1917 Feb 1	16:00	Thelus	B.E.2e (6742)	No. 16 RFC	22	19	Lt. P. W. Murray (died)	Lt. T. D. McRae (died)	5
1917 Feb 14	12:00	Loos	B.E.2d (6231)	No. 2 RFC	23	20	Lt. C. D. Bennet (wd; p.o.w.)	2nd/Lt. H. A. Croft (killed)	
1917 Feb 14	16:45	Mazingarbe	F.E.2	No 20 RFC	24	21	Capt. H. E. Hartney (wounded)	Lt. W. T. Jourden (wounded)	
1917 Mar 3	17:00	Souchez	B.E.2c	No. 16 RFC	25	24	C. M. G. Libby	G. J. A. Brichta	
1917 Mar 4	12:50	North of Loos	B.E.2d (5785)	No. 2 RFC	26	23	Sgt. J. E. Prance	Lt. J. E. B. Crosbee	6
1917 Mar 4	16:20	Acheville	Sopwith 1 1/2 (A1108)	No. 43 RFC	27	22	Lt. H. J. Green (killed)	Lt. W. Reid (killed)	
1917 Mar 9	11:55	Bailleul	D.H.2 (A2571)	No. 29	28	25	Lt. A. W. Pearson (killed)		
1917 Mar 11	12:00	Vimy	B.E.2d (6232)	No. 2 RFC	29	26	2nd/Lt. J. Smith (killed)	Lt. E. Byrne (killed)	
1917 Mar 17	11:30	Oppy	F.E.2b (A5439)	No. 25 RFC	30	27	Lt. A. E. Boultbee (killed)	Air/Mech. F. King (killed)	
1917 Mar 17	17:00	Vimy	B.E.2c (2814)	No. 16 RFC	31	28	2nd/Lt. G. M. Watt (killed)	Sgt. F. A. Howlett (killed)	
1917 Mar 21	17:30	N of La Neuville	B.E.2c (A3154)	No. 16 RFC	32	29	Sgt. S. H. Quicke (killed)	2nd/Lt. W. J. Lidsey (killed)	
1917 Mar 24	11:55	Givenchy	Spad S.7 (A6706)	RFC	33	30	Lt. R. P. Baker (wd; p.o.w.)		
1917 Mar 25	08:20	Tilloy	Nieuport 17 (A6689)	No. 29 RFC	34	31	2nd/Lt. C. G. Gilbert (p.o.w.)		
1917 Apr 2	08:35	Farbus	B.E.2d (5841)	RFC	35	32	Lt. J. C. Powell (killed)	Air/Mech. P. Bonner (killed)	
1917 Apr 2	11:15	Givenchy	Sopwith 1 1/2 (A2401)	No. 43 RFC	36	33	2nd/Lt. P. Warren (p.o.w.)	Sgt. R. Dunn (killed)	
1917 Apr 3	16:15	Lens	F.E.2d (A6382)	No. 25 RFC	37	34	2nd/Lt. D. P. McDonald (wd; p.o.w.)	2nd/Lt. J. I. M. O'Beirne (killed)	
1917 Apr 5	11:15	Lembras	Bristol F.2A (A3340)	No. 48 RFC	38	35	Lt. A. M. Leckler (wd; p.o.w.)	Lt. H. D. K. George (died)	
1917 Apr 5	11:30	Quincy	Bristol F.2A (A3343)	No. 48 RFC	39	36	Lt. A. T. Adams (wd; p.o.w.)	Lt. D. J. Stewart (p.o.w.)	
1917 Apr 7	17:45	Mercatel	Nieuport 17 (A6645)	No. 60 RFC	40	37	2nd/Lt. G. O. Smart (killed)		
1917 Apr 8	11:40	Farbus	Sopwith 1 1/2 (A2406)	No. 43 RFC	41	38	Lt. J. S. Heagerty (wd; p.o.w.)	Lt. L. H. Cantle (killed)	
1917 Apr 8	16:40	Vimy	B.E.2e (A2815)	No. 16 RFC	42	39	2nd/Lt. K. I. Mackensie (killed)	2nd/Lt. G. Everingham (killed)	
1917 Apr 11	09:25	Willerval	B.E.2c (2501)	No. 13 RFC	43	40	Lt. E. C. E. Derwin (wounded)	Gnr. H. Pierson (wounded)	
1917 Apr 13	08:58	Vitry/Brebieres	R.E.8 (A3190)	No. 59 RFC	44	41	Capt. J. Stuart (killed)	Lt. M. H. Wood (killed)	
1917 Apr 13	12:45	Monchy/Feuchy	F.E.2b	No. 25 RFC	45	42	Sgt. J. Cunliffe	2 Air/Mech. W. J. Bolton	
1917 Apr 13	19:35	Henin-Lietard	F.E.2b (4997)	No. 25 RFC	46	43	2nd/Lt. A. H. Bates (killed)	Sgt. W. A. Barnes (killed)	
1917 Apr 14	09:15	Bois Bernard	Nieuport 17 (A6796)	No. 60 RFC	47	44	Lt. W. O. Russell (p.o.w.)		
1917 Apr 16	17:30	Bailleul/Cavrelle	B.E.2c	RFC	48	45	Lt. W. Green (wounded)	Lt. C. E. Wilson (killed)	

DATE	TIME	LOCATION	AIRCRAFT	SQUADRON	VICTORY NO.	OFFICIAL SCORE	PILOT	OBSERVER	NOTES
1917 Apr 22	17:10	Lagnicourt	F.E.2b (7020)	RFC	49	46	Lt. W. F. Fletcher (wounded)	Lt. W. Franklin (wounded)	
1917 Apr 23	12:05	Mericourt	B.E.2e (A3168)	RFC	50	47	2nd/Lt. E. A. Welch (killed)	Sgt. A. Tollervey (killed)	
1917 Apr 28	09:30	East of Pelves	B.E.2e (7221)	RFC	51	48	Lt. R. W. Follit (killed)	2nd/Lt. F. J. Kirkham (wd; p.o.w.)	
1917 Apr 29	12:05	Lecluse	Spad S.7 (B1573)	No. 19 RFC	52	49	Lt. R. Applin (killed)		
1917 Apr 29	16:55	SW of Inchy Pariville	F.E.2b (4898)	No. 18 RFC	53	50	Sgt. G. Stead (killed)	Cpl. A. Beebee (killed)	
1917 Apr 29	19:25	Roeux	B.E.2d	No. 12 RFC	54	51	D. E. Davis	G. H. Rathbone	
1917 Apr 29	19:40	Billy-Montigny	Nieuport 17 (A6745)	No. 40 RFC	55	52	Capt. F. L. Barwell (killed)		
1917 June 18	13:15	Strugwe	R.E.8	RFC	56	53	Lt. R. W. Ellis (killed)	Lt. H. C. Barlow (killed)	
1917 June 23	21:30	North of Ypres	Spad S.7	Belgian	57	54	Unidentified		
1917 June 25	18:40	Le Bizet	R.E.8	RFC	58	56	Lt. L. S. Bowman (killed)	2nd/Lt. J. E. Power-Clutterbuck (killed)	
1917 June 26	21:10	Kebergmelen	D.H.4	No. 57 RFC	59	55	R. N. Mearns	N. C. McNaughton	
1917 July 2	10:20	Deulemont	R.E.8 (A3538)	No. 53 RFC	60	57	Sgt. H. A. Wheatley (killed)	2nd/Lt. F. J. Pasco (killed)	
1917 Aug 16	Not Known	Houthulster	Nieuport 17	RFC	61	58	Unidentified		
1917 Aug 26	07:30	Poel-capelle	Spad S.7 (B3492)	No. 19 RFC	62	59	2nd/Lt. C. P. Williams (killed)		
1917 Sept 1	07:50	Zonnebeke	R.E.8	RFC	63	60	2nd/Lt. J. B. C. Madge (wd; p.o.w.)	2nd/Lt. W. Kember (killed)	8
1917 Sept 3	07:35	Bousbecque	Sopwith Pup (B1795)	RFC	64	61	Lt. A. F. Bird (p.o.w.)		8
1917 Nov 23	14:00	Bourlon Wood	D.H.5 (A9299)	No. 64 RFC	65	62	Lt. J. A. V. Boddy (wounded)		9
1917 Nov 30	14:30	Moevres	S.E.5a (B40)	RFC	66	63	Capt. P. T. Townsend (killed)		9
1918 Mar 12	11:10	Nauroy	Bristol F.2B (B1251)	No. 62 RFC	67	64	Lt. L. C. F. Clutterbuck (p.o.w.)	2nd/Lt. H. J. Sparks (wd; p.o.w.)	10
1918 Mar 13	10:35	Gonnelieu/Banteaux	Sopwith Camel (B5590)	No. 73 RFC	68	65	2nd/Lt. J. M. L. Millett (killed)		10
1918 Mar 18	11:15	Andigny	Sopwith Camel (B5243)	No. 54 RFC	69	66	Lt. W. G. Ivamy (p.o.w.)		10
1918 Mar 24	14:45	Combles	S.E.5a (C5389)	No. 56 RFC	70	67	2nd/Lt. W. Porter (killed)		11
1918 Mar 25	15:55	Contal-maison	Sopwith Camel (C1582)	No. 3 RFC	71	68	2nd/Lt. D. Cameron (killed)		11
1918 Mar 26	16:45	Contal-maison	Sopwith Camel	RFC	72	69	2nd/Lt. W. Knox (killed)		11
1918 Mar 26	17:00	Albert	R.E.8 (B742)	No. 15 RFC	73	70	2nd/Lt. V. J. Reading (killed)	2nd/Lt. M. Leggat (killed)	11
1918 Mar 27	09:00	Aveloy	Sopwith Camel (C8234)	No. 70 RFC	74	71	Lt. H. W. Ransom (killed)		12
1918 Mar 27	16:30	Foucau-court	Bristol F.2B (B1156)	No. 20 RFC	75	72	Capt. K. R. Kirkham (p.o.w.)	Capt. J. H. Hedley (p.o.w.)	11
1918 Mar 27	16:35	Chuignolles	Bristol F.2B (B1332)	No. 11 RFC	76	73	Capt. H. R. Child (killed)	Lt. A Reeve (killed)	11
1918 Mar 28	12:30	Mericourt	A.W.F.K.8 (C8444)	No. 82 RFC	77	74	2nd/Lt. J. B. Taylor (killed)	2nd/Lt. E. Betley (killed)	12
1918 Apr 2	12:30	Moreuil	R.E.8 (A3868)	No. 52 RAF	78	75	2nd/Lt. E. D. Jones (killed)	2nd/Lt. R. F. Newton (killed)	11
1918 Apr 6	15:45	Villers-Brettoneaux	Sopwith Camel (D6491)	No. 46 RAF	79	76	Capt. S. P. Smith (killed)		12
1918 Apr 7	11:30	Hangard	S.E.5a (C1083)	No. 1 RAF	80	77	Capt. G. B. Moore (killed)		11
1918 Apr 7	12:05	Villers-Brettoneaux	Spad S.7	RAF	81	78	Unidentified		11
1918 Apr 20	18:40	Bois-de-Hamel	Sopwith Camel (D6439)	No. 3 RAF	82	79	Maj. R. Raymond-Barker (killed)		13
1918 Apr 20	18:43	Villers-Brettoneaux	Sopwith Camel (B7393)	No. 3 RAF	83	80	2nd/Lt. D. G. Lewis (wd; p.o.w.)		13

Notes

1: Von Richthofen shot down this aircraft while serving as an observer and because it fell on the British side of the lines it was not possible to recover evidence for confirmation.

2: This victory was achieved while von Richthofen was operating as a pilot and using a machine gun mounted to the upper wing.

3: The first victory achieved flying an Albatros D-class single-seat scout.

4: Because another pilot also put in a claim for this aircraft it was not confirmed as one of von Richthofen's kills. All the evidence suggests, however, that he was the victor.

5: This was the only official victory obtained by von Richthofen while flying a Halberstadt, which he had temporarily taken up after the lower wing on his Albatros D.III cracked on January 24, 1917.

6: All other books quote the victims as F/Sgt. R. J. Moody and 2nd/Lt. E. E. Horn flying B. E. 2d 6252 from No. 8 Sqdn. RFC. However, research by Peter Wright published in Cross & Cockade Vol. 14. pages 122-125, suggests otherwise.

7: This was the first victory scored by von Richthofen flying one of the new Albatros D.V series single-seat scouts.

8: Victories scored while flying Fokker Dr. I FI 102/17.

9: These two victories were scored on Albatros D.V aircraft during the period when the Dr. I was grounded pending an investigation into a spate of wing failures.

10: Victories scored flying Fokker Dr. I 152/17.

11: Victories scored while flying Fokker Dr. I 477/17.

12: Victories scored while flying Fokker Dr. I 127/17.

13: Victories scored while flying Fokker Dr. I 425/17.

Manfred von Richthofen was among the first of the select few given charge of the new Albatros biplane fighting scout when it appeared in late summer 1916. He was to score the majority of his 80 confirmed victories with aircraft from this marquee, switching to a Fokker Dr.I in September 1917, when he scored his 60th victory. It was on one of the early Albatros D.II biplanes that he scored his first officially credited victory - on September 17, 1916, in an aircraft believed to carry the serial number 481/16 or 491/16.

The Albatros biplane scouts, in effect, replaced the highly successful Fokker E.I-IV monoplanes and these in turn were superseded, albeit briefly, by the Fokker triplane. When the Fokker triplane fell from favour and triplanes in general were no longer coveted, the Albatros prevailed in competition with later types like the Fokker D.VII and in early summer 1918 more than 1,000 D.V and D.Va were still in service. In this way, some believe the Albatros biplane scouts to have been the most successful because they were prominent in numbers and performance from summer 1916, until the end of the war in November 1918.

In all, about 4,200 Albatros biplane scouts were ordered and the D.Va was used after the 1919 peace treaty to equip aerial 'police' units. Albatros was one of the oldest German aeroplane makers, the first product emerging in 1910 just three years after the first flight of a European powered aircraft. Tasked with designing an aircraft to counter the agile British Airco D.H.2 and the French Nieuport biplane, both of which adopted rotary engines, Robert Thelen and Schubert came up with a

sturdy biplane of conventional appearance with an in-line engine. Selected for its power, Thelen stipulated a 160 hp Mercedes or a 150 hp Benz engine. The new British and French scouts initially used engines of 100 hp and 80 hp, respectively, similar in performance to the engines used for the Fokker monoplanes.

Of semi-monocoque construction, the D.I had a conventional wing structure of approximately equal span but the revolutionary fuselage was a major feature of the new design. Built up on six spruce longerons, ply formers supported three-ply wood panels tacked on to form the exterior surface. The rounded nose followed smoothly on to a slab-sided fuselage and a knife-edge section at the rear where it met the streamlined tail. The vertical fin supporting the rudder was mirrored by a smaller, lower fin formed by a fairing over the tail skid. The horizontal tail was reminiscent of the type first seen on the Albatros C.V and C.VII two-seat reconnaissance aircraft and would be a recognition feature of subsequent single-seat scouts from this manufacturer.

The fabric covered wings were formed from two box spars forward and wire trailing edge aft with a large cut-out to facilitate the view above and forward. Two centre-section cabane struts met at the upper wing attachment point giving an inverted 'V' appearance from the front or rear. The D.II followed the D.I within a few weeks, when pilots complained about the lack of forward visibility which forced modifications. The relatively high upper wing position of the D.I was changed by lowering it 5.5 inches, and replacing the existing cabane strut design with an 'N' shaped centre-section

strut arrangement, modifications which improved the forward view.

The smooth appearance of the streamlined fuselage was disturbed by the bulky shape of two large Windhoff radiators, one either side of the nose section behind the engine mounting. Decreasing the gap between the wings increased air turbulence over these clumsy protruberances and this adversely affected the aircraft's performance. Thelen replaced the Windhoffs with a central, flush mounted radiator in the centre-section of the upper wing. Consequently, some D.II had the side-mounted radiators while later models had the modified configuration.

Armament comprised two 7.92-mm Maxim machine guns, most of which were more popularly called Spandau from the name of the place where they were built. Set to fire along each side of the cylinder heads, the guns were fed with 500 round belts of ammunition carried on webbing, ejecting cases through chutes around the gun breeches. Line of sight was along the top of the fuselage and engine, the target being positioned between the converging barrels of the two guns.

It is believed that 50 D.I were followed in production by approximately 275 D.II before the D.III was introduced in January 1917. By the end of the year the earlier models had virtually disappeared. Several famous pilots flew the D.I and the D.II, including Oswald Boelcke who led the first D.I patrol on September 17, 1916, and was killed in one on October 28, 1916. It was while flying a D.II that Manfred von Richthofen shot down and killed the British pilot Maj. Lanoe Hawker on November 23, 1916, as well as others.

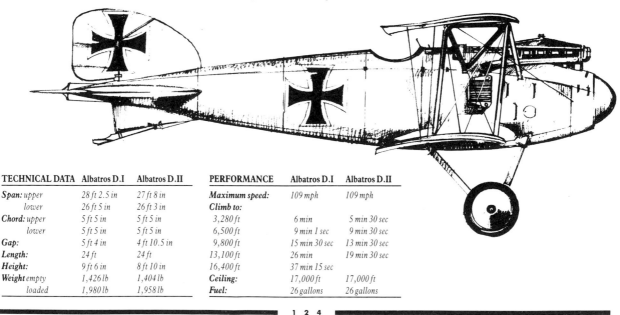

TECHNICAL DATA	Albatros D.I	Albatros D.II
Span: upper	28 ft 2.5 in	27 ft 8 in
lower	26 ft 5 in	26 ft 3 in
Chord: upper	5 ft 5 in	5 ft 5 in
lower	5 ft 5 in	5 ft 5 in
Gap:	5 ft 4 in	4 ft 10.5 in
Length:	24 ft	24 ft
Height:	9 ft 6 in	8 ft 10 in
Weight empty	1,426 lb	1,404 lb
loaded	1,980 lb	1,958 lb

PERFORMANCE	Albatros D.I	Albatros D.II
Maximum speed:	109 mph	109 mph
Climb to:		
3,280 ft	6 min	5 min 30 sec
6,500 ft	9 min 1 sec	9 min 30 sec
9,800 ft	15 min 30 sec	13 min 30 sec
13,100 ft	26 min	19 min 30 sec
16,400 ft	37 min 15 sec	
Ceiling:	17,000 ft	17,000 ft
Fuel:	26 gallons	26 gallons

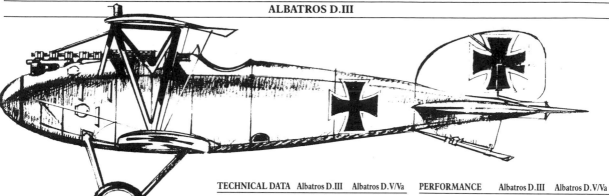

TECHNICAL DATA	Albatros D.III	Albatros D.V/Va		PERFORMANCE	Albatros D.III	Albatros D.V/Va
Span: *upper*	*29 ft 6.5 in*	*29 ft 6.5 in*		**Maximum speed:**	*108 mph*	*107 mph*
lower	*28 ft 8 in*	*28 ft 8 in*		**Climb to:**		
Chord: *upper*	*4 ft 10 in*	*4 ft 10 in*		*3,280 ft*	*3 min 20 sec*	*4 min 00 sec*
lower	*3 ft 8 in*	*3 ft 8 in*		*6,500 ft*	*8 min 48 sec*	
Gap:	*5 ft 1 in*	*4 ft 10/8.5 in*		*9,800 ft*	*12 min 01 sec*	*14 min 47 sec*
Length:	*24 ft*	*24 ft*		*13,100 ft*	*18 min 45 sec*	*22 min 45 sec*
Height:	*9 ft 10 in*	*9 ft 6/4.5 in*		**16,400 ft**	*28 min 48 sec*	*35 min 00 sec*
Weight: *empty*	*1,457 lb*	*1,496/1,515 lb*		**Ceiling:**	*18,000 ft*	*20,500 ft*
loaded	*1,953 lb*	*2,013/2,066 lb*		**Fuel:**	*24 gallons*	*25 gallons*

Seeking improved performance and better handling in a dog-fight, the Albatros factory produced a modified D.II at the end of 1916. The compression ratio of the Mercedes engine was increased to produce 170 hp, the biplane arrangement was given a sesquiplane configuration and the span of the upper wing was increased but the fuselage of the D.II was retained. The net effect was to increase overall performance, significantly improve visibility all around, and provide the German Air Service with one of its most successful fighting aircraft of the period. Known as the D.III, about 1,340 were built before it was replaced by the D.V which first appeared in May 1917.

Compared with earlier Albatros single-seat scouts, the principal visual feature of the D.III was the high degree of sweep-back on all four wing tips with inverse taper on the ailerons and the true sesquiplane appearance of the biplane. The chord of the lower wing was reduced considerably and built on a single spar while the upper wing had two forward box spars connected to the leading edge by a plywood strip. The wing gap was 5 ft 1 in, 2.5 greater than the wing gap on the D.II.

Inspiration for the new wing design came from captured French built Nieuport scouts which first popularised the sesquiplane configuration among German manufacturers. One German firm, Siemens-Schuckert, built an almost exact copy of the Nieuport called the D.I, of which less than 100 were actually constructed. German aircraft builders were encouraged to copy the Nieuport wing because it proved to impart a useful manoeuvrability to the aircraft.

It had the added advantage of drastically

reducing the surface area of the lower wing, improving downward visibility. There was a price for this, however, and structural failure was a continuous problem for the D.III and D.V series as high speed dives caused flexing of the lower wing section forward of the spar and subsequent collapse. Some late model D.III had a small auxiliary strut attached between the leading edge of the lower wing and the lower section of the forward leg of the 'V' shaped interplane strut. This effort at strengthening the lower wing was a partial success and had been introduced for the D.V/Va series.

Originally fitted with a Teeves and Braun radiator in the centre of the upper wing, later models carried a radiator offset to starboard which had the advantage of carrying the feed and return pipes further to one side of the engine cylinder line. This improved the forward view and also prevented the pilot being scalded by a jet of hot water released by an unlucky bullet hole. The 'N' shape centre section and 'V' shaped interplane struts were of light steel tubing, the former splayed outward in a similar configuration to the D.II.

Designer Robert Thelen adopted the fuselage and tail of the D.I and D.II virtually without change and the D.III had the characteristic cross sections of that first generation Albatros scout. From a round nose section where it met the spinner the cross section became slab-sided with top and bottom curves between the engine and rear fuselage, shaped to a flat knife-edge at the tail. As with the earlier series, the tail was an integral part of the rear fuselage with three-ply covering over a wooden frame. The undercarriage was the same as that designed

for the earlier series, as was the armament. The D.III became operational in January 1917. It arrived at the right time to give the German Air Service temporary ascendency over existing Allied aircraft and turned spring 1917 into a virtual orgy of destruction. Von Richthofen did well flying the D.III although the tendency of the aircraft's lower wing to break up was of constant concern and caused him to switch to the Halberstadt D.II for a period. Nevertheless, even when the D.V series was introduced in mid-1917, the D.III continued in parallel production through early 1918.

Several D.III adopted modifications applied to the D.V. Some, for instance, had the auxiliary strengthening strut mentioned earlier, others had the rounded rudder rather than the type with a straight trailing edge previously fitted to the D.I and D.II. It is therefore difficult to be dogmatic about identification of specific aircraft when only portions of the airframe are visible. The fuselage of the D.V, however, was completely different in design and shape and that would be a key feature of the later type.

The Austrian Oeffag company designed and built a version of the D.III capable of taking alternative engines. With either the 185 hp or 200 hp Austro-Daimler engine they used the same nose section as the standard Albatros factory model, but with the more powerful 225 hp engine they redesigned the front end. Being a much larger engine the fuselage was re-shaped and given a rounded nose without a spinner, the propeller being attached directly in front of the fuselage. These engines increased the performance of the D.III and raised the top speed.

There was no production Albatros D.IV, that type number being assigned to a specially developed test bed for the geared 160 hp Mercedes engine. Built in 1917, the D.IV never evolved to a production design largely because of problems with the engine, but it was the most streamlined Albatros built. With a completely enclosed engine, tapered head rest, rounded rudder and a wing arrangement reminiscent of the D.I and D.II it looked capable but performance was poor. Nevertheless, the single example built soldiered on doing engine tests until early 1918.

Albatros had produced the D.III by taking the fuselage of the D.I/D.II and fitting to it a completely new wing design. They produced the D.V by taking the wings of the D.III and attaching them to a completely new fuselage. New and improved Allied scouts were proving more than a challenge to the D.III and the company came up with a series of refinements rather than a radical solution to impending obsolescence. Although the D.V was not a major improvement on its predecessor it provided an opportunity to tidy up the design and produce the definitive production model.

Instead of flat sides with rounded top and bottom, the new fuselage had a smooth, streamlined, elliptical cross section. Construction was from a series of formers and longerons without internal bracing covered by plywood panels in a similar manner to the previous design. Wider than the fuselage of the D.III, that of the D.V had an extra longeron each side. The factory provided a head rest of substantial size but this was frequently

removed by pilots to improve visibility to the rear. The D.V/Va also had the rounded rudder trailing edge first introduced on late model D.III scouts while the tail skid had a fabric fairing like previous models but with an angled rake of 45 deg.

Because the fuselage had an elliptical cross section, Albatros fitted stubs to the belly where the lower wing was attached, thus permitting full interchangeability of D.III wings with D.V models. Moreover, the wing gap was reduced to 4 ft 10 in, almost exactly that of the D.II. Unique to D.V wings, however, was the aileron control arrangement. The D.III control wire ran from the aileron crank down to the lower wing directly behind the 'V' interplane strut, thence along the interior of the wing to the fuselage. On the D.V, the wire running from a control horn on the aileron was passed along the interior of the upper wing to the centre section from which point it was carried down to the fuselage.

When Albatros produced the derivative D.Va, they reverted to the old style of aileron control and the absence of control horns is the only positive way to identify this type. The pilot of a D.V stood a reasonable chance of bringing his aircraft down safely if the lower wing failed because the aileron control was carried through the upper wing. The D.Va reversed this advantage. In-flight wing failure would collapse the aileron controls.

At least one D.V was reported by British air ace James Byford McCudden as having two 'V' interplane struts each side, presumably to inhibit structural failure, but this has never

been confirmed. Internally, the airframe was strengthened in the D.Va and the headrests were permanently removed. Another feature was the wing gap, reduced to 4 ft 8.5 in on the D.Va.

The engine fitted to the D.V series was the standard 160 hp Mercedes D.III boosted to a maximum 180 hp by oversize pistons and a high compression ratio. Some were fitted with the 220 hp Mercedes and even the 225 hp Benz engine but this latter version was specifically intended for high altitude work and never adopted as standard. Fitted with a 185 hp BMW IIIa engine, one D.Va achieved an uncorrected altitude of 34,450 ft on February 6, 1918. With the standard, high compression engine and the aircraft's additional weight the D.V had a performance which stressed the wing design, resulting in a spate of structural failures when the type was introduced.

The D.V entered service with the Jagdstaffeln during May 1917, barely five months after the introduction of the D.III. The D.Va followed in October. In all, 2,512 were built, 1,612 were the Va derivative. The aircraft became the standard mount for all Germany's leading air aces and formed the backbone of single-seat scout units on the Western Front. In its operational life, between the first Albatros D.I patrol on September 17, 1916, and the Armistice on November 11, 1918, the Albatros single-seat scout was a firm favourite. Not without flaw, it was a generally robust if somewhat unwieldy warplane but many of Germany's leading fighter pilots secured the majority of their kills on Albatros scouts.

FOKKER D.III

Flown by von Richthofen during his time at Jagdstaffel 2 awaiting delivery of an Albatros D.I, the Fokker D.III evolved from the D.II single engine two-bay biplane which first entered service in July 1916. Responding to new and superior Allied aircraft that made their monoplanes increasingly outdated, the Dutch born aircraft manufacturer Anthony Fokker produced a biplane to replace the monoplanes in service. But it too was obsolete before it entered service and the Albatros scouts gained increasing favour.

Probably because of the high value placed on Fokker's monoplanes, Oswald Boelcke flew a D.III which he had been given on September 1, 1916. With it he was to score six victories in just over two weeks before switching to an Albatros D.I which had superior performance. The Fokker D.III made but a brief bid for fame. Only 159 were built and by early 1917 only a handful remained.

Fokker tried to retain the advantage of the monoplane by designing the D.III to carry a

rotary engine like its predecessors. Powered by a 160 hp twin-row, fourteen cylinder, Oberursel which had been used in the last Fokker monoplane type, the D.III had twin-bay wings braced internally and externally. The fuselage and tail was of wire braced tubular steel construction and two synchronised machine guns were fitted to the top decking of the nose section just behind a deep cowl for the rotary engine.

TECHNICAL DATA	Fokker D.II	PERFORMANCE	Fokker D.II
Span: upper	28 ft 8 in	**Maximum speed:**	93 mph
lower	28 ft 8 in	**Climb to:**	
Chord: upper	3 ft 10.5 in	3,280 ft	3 min
lower	3 ft 10.5 in	6,500 ft	8 min
Gap:	4 ft 5 in	9,800 ft	15 min
Length:	20 ft 11 in	13,100 ft	24 min
Height:	8 ft 3.5 in	**Ceiling:**	13,100 ft
Weight: empty	845 lb	**Endurance:**	1.5 hours
loaded	1,267 lb		

FOKKER Dr.I

Made famous by von Richthofen, the diminutive Fokker Dr.I triplane was built in response to a belief that three wings would bestow greater manoeuvrability to an aircraft than a biplane could. Seduced into this design philosophy by the unpredicted success of the Sopwith Triplane, Anthony Fokker visited Jagdstaffel 11 in April 1917, and was taken by von Richthofen to see a Sopwith Triplane in flight over the trenches. Von Richthofen stressed to Fokker the urgency of producing an agile fighter at least the equal of the new Allied aircraft.

For long there has been a belief that Fokker and a team led by Reinhold Platz designed the Dr.I from technical knowledge of the Sopwith Triplane. This is not true. Some had been captured, but not before July did German aircraft manufacturers receive a technical report describing the Sopwith design. By that time Fokker was well under way with his V.3 design. It evolved from a line of *verspannungslos* (wing with no internal bracing) cantilever designs originated by Reinhold Platz with the V.1 in 1916. With fabric covered wooden hoops and stringers, the fuselage of the V.1 supported a full cantilever biplane without interplane struts.

The V.3 had three cantilever wings. Of equal span, the lower two wings were attached to the bottom and top of the forward fuselage respectively, while the top wing had a greater span and was supported by a pair of inverse 'V' cabane struts. The aircraft was powered by a 100 hp Oberursel rotary and had a span of 118 ft with a length of almost 19 ft. Changes

introduced after flight tests produced the V.4 which became the definitive Fokker triplane, designated F.I for a brief period before the permanent designation Dr.I. The first production order was granted July 14, 1917, and the Dr.I passed its acceptance tests on August 16. The first two were taken to Jagdgeschwader Nr.1 at Courtrai on the 21st.

The fuselage and tail was of welded steel tube construction made rigid with transverse bracing. Most of the fuselage was covered with fabric but the circular cross section of the engine firewall was merged with the square cross section of the mid and aft fuselage by a triangular shaped fillet made of plywood. Power was provided by a 110 hp Le Rhone or Oberursel rotary engine partly enclosed by a cowl perforated by two circular, or elongated, cutouts. Giving the aircraft the appearance of a face when seen front on, Werner Voss did the obvious and painted eyes, eyebrows and a moustache on the front of the third aircraft (103/17).

The cantilever wings were of equal chord and construction but the lower wing had a span of 18 ft 9 in, the middle wing a span of 20 ft 6 in and the top wing a span of 22 ft 1 in, or 23 ft 7 in including the overhung aileron sections. Each wing was built on a deep, wooden box spar with plywood ribs and plywood covering from the leading edge back to the spar. The rest was fabric covered. In addition, the undercarriage axle fairing had a chord of 25 in and a span of 4 ft 9 in, also of considerable depth. The top wing was attached to the forward fuselage by two inverted centre section

'V' struts splayed outward so that the apex converged at the spar position.

Flight controls included balanced ailerons on the top wing only, with control cables running along the spar line and down to the cockpit in the vicinity of the centre section struts. The familar comma-shaped Fokker rudder was fitted without a vertical tail while the horizontal tail took the form of a triangular shape in plan including elevators. A characteristic design change on the Dr.I compared to the V.3 was the provision of a single 'I' strut each side connecting all three wings. This was not strictly necessary but it did prevent flexing and flutter in a dive. After the first few had been delivered, ash skids were attached to each wing tip.

Armament comprised twin Spandau machine guns in front of the pilot while instruments included a tachometer, fuel pressure gauge, an ammeter and a compass set on a pedestal to one side of the pilot's legs. The control stick incorporated a double hand grip with an auxiliary throttle lever and separate buttons for firing each gun. It also provided an engine cutout switch. The seat was of welded steel construction, the whole covered with leather, and could be adjusted for height and position. Barely two months after the Dr.I began operations, Lt. Heinrich Gontermann was killed when on October 29, 1917, the upper wing of his triplane, 115/17, collapsed. Two days later Dr.I 121/17 flown by Lt. Pastor also lost its top wing and the type was grounded. Fokker was notified on November 28 that tests on a strengthened wing had proved satisfactory and the ban was subsequently lifted. Fokker received an initial order for 320 triplanes and expected to build many more but the month during which the type was grounded proved fatal for the triplane's future prospects. No more were ordered and Anthony Fokker turned his efforts to other designs, one of which emerged as the D.VII.

Although von Richthofen flew a triplane on operations for a total of only six weeks out of his three years as an aviator, scoring only 19 of his 80 confirmed victories in a Dr.I, he liked the type and used it well. Although at least 10 mph slower than the Albatros, it had a good climb rate, handled superbly and was very manoeuvrable. These qualities were best interpreted by a gifted pilot like Werner Voss. Between early February and mid-March 1918,

three more Dr.Is were lost to structural failure, two of which were probably damaged in combat. Another was lost in May due to poor workmanship, the month the last of 320 was delivered.

By summer 1918, the Dr.I was becoming a rarity. The D.VII was replacing them in large numbers. Even when it entered service the triplane had been outclassed by the better Allied aircraft like the Sopwith Camel and the Spad 13. Capable of carrying the fight to ever increasing altitudes, the Allies had aircraft superior to the triplane, which was at least 35 mph slower than the Spad 13 at 13,000 ft. Air crew in British day bombers like the D.H.4 frequently outran the triplane. Only in the hands of experienced or successful pilots did the triplane prove its worth.

TECHNICAL DATA	Fokker Dr.I
Span: top	23 ft 7 in
middle	20 ft 6 in
lower	18 ft 9 in
Chord: top	3 ft 3 in
middle	3 ft 3 in
lower	3 ft 3 in
Gap:	2 ft 5.5 in
Length:	19 ft
Height:	9 ft 1 in
Weight: empty	829 lb
loaded	1,259 lb

PERFORMANCE	Fokker Dr.I
Maximum speed:	97 mph
Climb to:	
3,280 ft	1 min 36 sec
6,500 ft	4 min 12 sec
9,800 ft	8 min 00 sec
13,100 ft	11 min 09 sec
16,400 ft	20 min 36 sec
Ceiling:	19,600 ft
Endurance:	1.5 hours
Fuel:	16.5 gallons

HALBERSTADT D.II

Von Richthofen may have flown aircraft of this type while awaiting Albatros D.I scouts when he first joined Jasta 2 in September 1916. The Halberstadter Flugzeugwerke, G.m.b.H., evolved out of the Deutsche Bristol-Werke which had been set up on February 28, 1912, half owned by the Bristol Aeroplane Company of England. When the Kaiser decreed that Germany should build fewer aircraft of foreign design, the licence manufacture of Bristol aircraft lapsed and a range of German designed monoplanes and biplanes emerged.

The 100 hp Mercedes engined D.I was produced in late 1915 and gave way to the D.II when a 120 hp engine of this types was fitted to

the compact biplane in 1916. With some modifications and a 120 hp Argus As II engine it was designated D.III. Armament comprised a single, fixed machine gun attached to the port side of the fuselage. In this form the aircraft achieved limited success but was seriously outclassed by early 1917.

Von Richthofen switched to a Halberstadt when structural failure to his Albatros lower wing caused more concern than usual. He scored his 19th official victory in a Halberstadt on February 1, 1917, but reverted to an Albatros thereafter. He found the Halberstadt highly manoeuvrable if somewhat unstable - characteristics that typify the classic fighting aeroplane.

TECHNICAL DATA	Halberstadt D.II
Span: upper	28 ft 10.5 in
lower	25 ft 11 in
Chord: top	5 ft
lower	5 ft
Gap:	4 ft 3
Length:	23 ft 11 in
Height:	8 ft 9 in
Weight: empty	1,234 lb
loaded	1,696 lb

PERFORMANCE	Halberstadt D.II
Maximum speed:	90 mph
Climb to:	
3,280 ft	4 min
6,500 ft	9 min
9,800 ft	15 min
Ceiling:	19,600 ft
Fuel:	18.5 gallons